The Treacle Stick

by Helen Butcher

QuercuS

****
QuercuS
John Roberts
67 Cliffe Way, Warwick CV34 5JG
Tel/Fax 01926 776363
****

The Treacle Stick

by Helen Butcher

ISBN 1 898136 18 1

First Published 1999

Preface

QuercuS specialises in publishing books about the western Midlands, or the area between the rivers Trent, Severn and Avon that geographers call the "Midland Triangle". Titles include *Midland Woods & Forests, Midland Rivers, Midland Ghosts & Hauntings, Midland Castles, Historic Houses & Gardens, Heart in my Boots, Coaching Days in the Midlands, Midland Murders & Mysteries, Midland Spirits & Spectres* and albums of pen and ink sketches of buildings in Hales Owen, Bromsgrove and Birmingham. Early in 1998 I brought out *Us Kids,* Carole Stafford's account of growing up in Ladywood between 1945 and 1960.

Helen Butcher had set down the story of her life in Ladywood, Aston and Erdington between 1917 and 1942 for the benefit of her family, particular her two grandsons. She was not thinking about having it published, but once the manuscript was finished, why not? Helen and her son Edward know our favourite Brummie historian, Carl Chinn, and he was encouraging. I was very happy that they asked me to publish *The Treacle Stick* because it is so interesting, and it fits very nicely with *Us Kids.*

The Author

HELEN BUTCHER was born Nellie Smith in Ladywood, Birmingham in 1917. After a difficult but not unusual backstreet childhood she left home to work as a maid at a large house in Barnt Green. All through her childhood, because she had no choice but accepting it as natural, Helen had to look after her younger sister, Florence. After jobs of all kinds she moved into factory work at Kynoch's in Witton, where she met her husband, George, a draftsman and later an engineer. After World War Two they moved to South Wales, but the family returned to the Midlands early in the 1960s. Helen was widdowed in 1988 and now lives in Droitwich.

*The author today
and at ages 11
and 16.*

Dedication

To my grandsons, Mark and Jeremy

The Cross Roads

One ship sails east,
The other sails west,
With the self same winds that blow,
T'is the set of the sails,
And not the gales,
That show us the way to go.

Dear Mark and Jeremy,

This little poem is not my work - I once had a brass plaque showing two ships going in different directions with those words beneath. I hope to prove to you how very true they are, because if I had I set my sails in the opposite direction to the one I chose, my life would have been quite different and I would not be telling my story to my two grandsons.

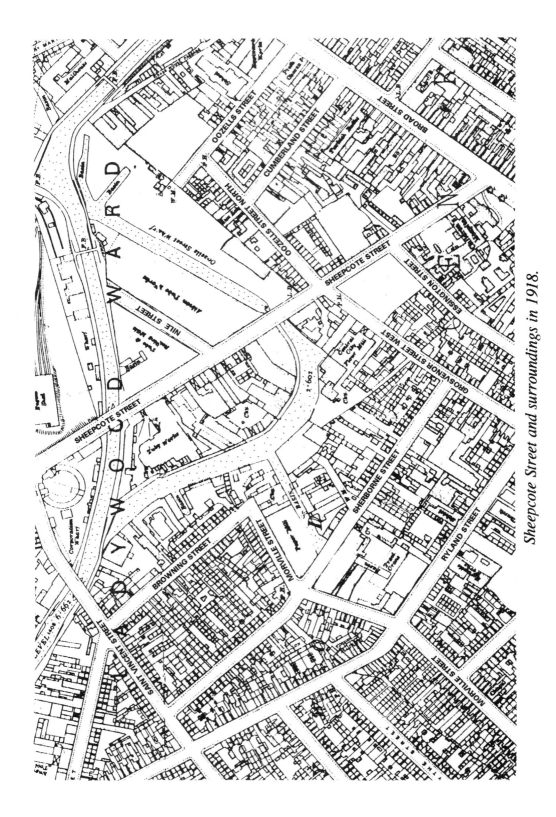

Sheepcote Street and surroundings in 1918.

Contents

Sheepcote Street

There was a milk shop in Sheepcote Street when we lived there in
the 1920s. It was owned by a Mrs Skinner who kept it spotlessly
clean, but the Public Health Inspectors of today would not have
liked the parrot hanging over the milk churns. That bird was
better than any burglar alarm. As soon as you set foot over the
doorstep he would let out a mighty squawk and go into his party
piece. This was loud and drawn out:

> *"MOTHER - YOU'RE WANTED."*

Mother would come from the living room behind the shop to serve
you. I never heard the parrot say anything but that one phrase.

All the hawkers and tradesmen shouted out their wares. You could
have a man with a handcart heaped with bananas shouting about
what he had to sell, and the price. Nearby there would be another
hawker with tomatoes yelling at the top of his lungs to outshout
the banana man. In competition would be the coalman with his
horse and cart, he also had a living to make. The rag and bone
men not only shouted but blew trumpets; they were not musical,
they just made a noise.

Added to the hawkers' cries, were the factory 'bulls', or sirens,
telling the workers when it was time to start work. The bull of
each works had its own distinctive sound so there was no excuse
for being late. Lateness was barely tolerated, and with so many
people out of work in the 1920s and early 30s there was always
somebody to step into your job. You were always on time and
you worked hard to keep it. My father was in the Army so at
least he had regular pay, even if it was not very much.

We lived in number 3/5 Sheepcote Street which was in a yard,
or court, near the junction with Broad Street. It was known
locally as the Big Yard and lay at right angles to Sheepcote
Street and parallel with Broad Street. These red brick and
slate roofed houses were called 'attic high', with a single
ground floor room, a bedroom and an attic. The attic had a
small fireplace and so did the bedroom, though we could not
ever afford to use them. The bedroom also held a cupboard
where we kept clothes.

Outside in the yard was a single water tap which supplied us and the eight other families. There was a block of toilets, the dustbins and the 'brew house', which might once have been used for brewing beer but now housed washday equipment.

Under the house was a cellar where we kept the coal. When the 'suff' [drain] in the yard was blocked the water would seep into our cellar. Soon the damp would rise up the walls and the snails would follow with the 'black bats' [beetles], so food was kept in a cupboard which hung in the living room. This also kept it safe from the mice, though Minnie, the cat, ran that department.

She was as good as any mousetrap and cheaper than the cheese which was used to bait them. We ate the cheese and Minnie had to be satisfied with a diet of scrapings from our plates. They were wiped so clean that even the roses in the pattern had faded. Minnie lived to the age of 10 but grieved after my father's death and just lay around, so she was put to sleep. I don't suppose anyone thought that perhaps she was not getting enough to eat. Domestic pets came off second best in those times. The money from the Board of Guardians did not allow for 'feeding of cat'.

Everything happened in our ground floor living room: cooking, eating, washing. We had a wooden settle which we called the squab, two chairs, and a wall fitment of two or three shelves over a cupboard which was screened off by a curtain. A rag rug covered some of the floor. These were made from miscellaneous scraps of material sewn onto a sack, so they were very colourful and practically indestructible. They also held an amazing amount of dust, there was plenty from the coal fire, and weighed a ton when you tried to shake them.

My mother's pride and joy was our table. She taught me to scrub it along the grain and, Lord help me, if I started to scrub in circles I would get a punch wherever her hand made contact. Soap was not used for this type of wood but a slab of hard substance called bath brick. That table really was white, 'Fit to eat off,' Mother would say.

Over the fireplace was a shelf draped along the edges with a length of chenille velvet, which was held in place by ornamental brasses screwed into the wood. Along the whole length of the fringe ran a double brass chain. Friday was brasses cleaning day and fish day. I hated fish but loved to do the brasses. We were poor but clean.

On the fireplace shelf were some vases with pictures of pretty ladies which were made not of china, but tin, and an 'alerum' clock. It was an alarm clock really, with a little bell on top, but we called it the alerum. Then there was a Mazzawatte tea caddy with oriental views. Living among such treasures gave me an appreciation of 'things' and a need to have them around me, which probably accounts for my shoe collection.

Kept with the treasures were our important documents, the rent book, insurance policies and the 'marriage lines'. If during a quarrel someone expressed doubt about your legitimacy, this document was flourished to silence all argument. It was a hard thing to have to live with, being a bastard. The poor child was completely innocent of any offence but usually rejected, even by its own family.

The most important thing in the house was the rent book with a 'C' on the right side of the page, denoting 'Clear'. There was no debt in our house because there would have been no way to pay if off, so the weekly 4 shillings and 8 pence [23p] was written down the pages with that precious 'C' beside it. Then there were the insurance policies which paid just enough money for a simple funeral. A decent burial was everyone's aim; no one wanted to be buried by the Parish. A pauper's burial would have been humiliating because you took the ignominy of poverty to the grave.

Our insurance premiums were scraped together come what may. I was nearly 2 years old before the insurance man would take me on his books at 2 pence [.8p] per week; he thought he was backing a loser. Florrie was accepted at a fortnight old, also at 2 pence. I kept those policies going for 60 years by which time they had become 'free', that is, all premiums due had been paid. You could keep them until you died or surrender them for cash. I surrendered mine but the proceeds would not have bought a tripe supper. Even so, Mother's policy produced enough to give her a decent funeral and a grave in the Church of England part of Witton Cemetery.

There has always been business for undertakers but infant mortality was so much higher in the early years of this century. Beneath the driving seat of the horsedrawn hearse was a small compartment for the coffins of babies.

My mother had had eleven children but only three survived to adulthood. Ted, the first born, died aged 67. Florrie was the last baby and reached 70. I came about seventh in the family and was

Helen and her grandson, Jeremy where Nile St lead to the canal (see next chapter) with rising NIA in the background.

On the north side of Sheepcote St is the modern idea of a 'yard'.

The canal transformed.

not expected to live through babyhood, but at 81 years of age
I am writing my autobiography.

It was the custom in the 1920s for little girls to act as bearers
at the funerals of small babies. We wore white frocks with a
deep, black sash around our waists. I was a bearer twice at 10
or 11 years of age. Today the thought of it fills me with horror,
but then it was an accepted duty and part of the pattern of life.
Thank goodness some fashions have died out. It did have one
benefit though, because it meant time off from school with a
good explanation for being absent.

Rosie Goode and I were bearers at one particular funeral.
She was a neighbour and we played together, so it was bound
to happen. It was and is still a fact that little girls, or big ones,
giggle. It could have been something that was said, I don't
know, but we started a giggle which soon became a laugh
and were both sent home in haste.

The newspaper seller who came up our yard was a very nice man,
but he was deaf, and for some reason always had a lump of cotton
wool in his ear. It was no use shouting to him from behind, you
had to meet him face to face. He had his own breath-saving way
of advertising the *Despatch* and the *Mail,* calling 'S'patchamail.'

On Sunday mornings a man came round with a little flat topped
donkey cart displaying newspapers and comics. He would call the
names of the newspapers, then shout, *Comic Cuts, Funny Wonder,
Butterfly, Jester, Chips.* I once had a comic from him, and what
joy those pages held. They did not last long because you would
soon read through them and go in search of someone to swap
with. One comic went a long way.

I preferred books to comics; that way you got the whole story.
I loved to read about the explorers, such as Mungo Park, Dr
Livingstone who was presumed, and Hudson (of Hudson Bay)
who was cast adrift with his little son by his rebellious crew
and never heard of again. Then there was Christopher Colum-
bus who did not really discover America but got the credit. My
favourite was Marco Polo who wrote about his exploits in China.

After school I would often go to the the public library in Edmund
Street in the middle of town, which was not very far away. I can't
remember having a library ticket but just presented myself at the

counter and asked if I could have a book. Although it was the Children's Library I was always alone and have no memory of seeing other children there, just shelf upon shelf of books. I loved being there because of the wonderful sense of freedom to choose any book I liked.

What a feast for someone who loved to read. Even if I was limited to the children's section there was plenty to suit all tastes and fancies. I once had a fancy to know about weaving, so I took a book on the subject. I had to take it straight back because my mother said it was not a proper book. What she meant was, it was not something I could read to her. I read books and newspapers to Mother because by this time her eyesight was failing. I wonder now whether she could read.

My favourite newspaper was *Thompson's Weekly* which was full of past murders. There were Jack the Ripper, Charlie Peace and a man named Lee - 'The Man They Couldn't Hang'. There was also a serial called 'The Bairn in the Snow' which always had a sad ending, but you had a week to cheer up before the next episode. This was always provided that Mrs Crutchly, or whichever neighbour you borrowed the paper from, did not forget to buy it.

I would also recite poems to my mother and sing the songs learned at school. Her favourite poem was 'The Blind Harper', and I recited it so often that she must have known it by heart. I could not know then what she surely must have known, that her eyesight was failing fast, and when she died aged 46 she was blind.

I would put all the feeling I could into that poem and the tears would roll down my cheeks. I always had top marks at school for recitation, especially of the stirring, patriotic stuff like 'Love of Country'.

> *Breathes there a man with soul so dead,*
> *Who never to himself hath said,*
> *This is my own - my native land, ... etc.,*

Another tear jerking poem was 'A Jacobite's Epitaph'. He had to leave England, 'Had thrown land, honour and wealth away' and gone to live in a foreign clime. So there he sat beside the River Arno crying and wanting to come back. What a mug, I thought, to go in the first place. If he had lived in Ladywood he would have known you couldn't throw anything away.

In Ladywood you did more than not throw things away, you scavenged whatever you could. Lads would go to the canal or 'cut' carrying a jam jar and a stick, to which was tied a piece of string with a bent pin in the end. I don't remember seeing any fish in the jam jars, but there were things to be got from canals, especially bits of coal which had fallen from the boats.

Alfred Flatley died in 1994 at the age of 91. He told me that as a boy he used to go with his father to the canal. His father would strip off his clothes and dive into the foul water in an effort to keep his family warm. If he did not find what he wanted in the mud they would be without a fire in the grate. So Alfred would stand on the towpath minding his father's clothes and holding a sack to catch the winnings.

With so much unemployment there was a great deal of real poverty. I wonder what my father would have said had he known, when his time in the Army was served, he would come home to such conditions, or what would later happen to his family. At the end of his service he received a pension which was paid every quarter day, and I remember going with him to Ladywood Police Station to get some necessary form signed.

But father died in March 1924 and the pension died with him, leaving my mother without means of any kind. She had three children to feed and clothe and there was no Widow's Pension Scheme until 1925, so we were destitute.

To survive you applied to The Board of Guardians, well fed, well dressed ladies and gentlemen who lived in Edgbaston, Barnt Green or Harborne. When they closed their office doors at the end of the day they said goodbye to the real world and retreated to a nice meal and a warming fire.

They were the Guardians of the Poor, with the power to dictate your destiny. They decided how much it would take each week to keep you in the poverty you were used to. Now you were 'on the Parish' and had to suffer its indignities, like presenting your grocery card to the shop assistant who could only give you the items stated. I remember how I felt handing over my card, with the other people in the shop looking and knowing I was 'on the parish'. I wanted to get out as fast as I could.

Not surprisingly, we did not have much variety in our diet. If the fire was alight in the morning we might have for breakfast a 'piece' [slice of bread] spread with margarine or lard and

toasted. If not I went to school clutching a piece which had
to suffice until dinner time. Dinner was from 12.00 to 2.00pm
and usually consisted of boiled meat, often breast of lamb, and
vegetables. Our dinner every Sunday was also breast of lamb,
but roasted in the little oven at the side of the fire and much
nicer. Sometimes we had rabbit, again, boiled.

A treat for us was bacon bones, and especially good if the
grocer's assistant had put in some knuckle bones. There was
some meat on those but not much to be had from the ribs. It
was the luck of the draw, or the shop assistant. Sometimes he
would let you pick your own from a box kept under the counter.
If I went home with a paper full of 'flat uns' I would get such
a shouting at, and if there were no bones in the shop I would
get the same. My mother used to say, 'You're the picture of
bad luck.' She must have been right because I never seemed
to please her. I could have grown into an introvert.

When I started school in 1922 at the age of 5 I took myself
to St Barnabas's in Ledsam Street. The primary school stood
behind the church and the senior school, with separate sections
for boys and girls, was on the opposite side of the road.

I liked school, especially English, reading, reciting poems and
composing stories. Then my imagination would run riot and I
always got good marks. History and geography suited and satisfied my enquiring mind and my eagerness to learn about far
off places, people and customs, and which explorer had first
been there.

Our school had five classes and we were taught in one large hall.
Two of the groups were separated only by being on different sides
of the hall. Curtains screened another class and also the headmistress and her desk, while two more classes were curtained off
at one end of the room. Apart from the big hall there was another
classroom on the front of the building overlooking Ledsam Street.

Things were not bad for me in lessons. I plodded on and made
some progress because I was eager and tried very hard to learn.
What I suffered from was the very strict rules about absence or
arriving late. If you were away for any length of time without
telling the headmistress, or sometimes if you did, the 'School
Board Man' from the Education Department would call at your
home to ask the reason. Almost the only acceptable excuse was

illness, and if you were ill you had to produce a certificate from the doctor.

If you had no certificate and were 'playing the wag' you were in trouble. That dreaded representative of authority would stalk your area to make sure you did not go far from home, so it would not be much fun if you could not do anything with your stolen time. If you managed to escape to 'Harborne Stiles', well away from home, to enjoy some freedom playing in the fields, the caning when you were found out and the hiding from your parents would have been worthwhile. Some boys, I never came across a girl 'playing the wag', were persistent truants and nothing seemed to cure them.

I lost a lot of time from school through my own illness and in having to take Mother to hospital for treatment. One day it would be the Eye Hospital in Church Street and another the Ear Nose & Throat in Barwick Street. I would get so upset each time Mother announced that I would miss school the next day. She always waited until just before I went to bed to tell me, and I would cry myself to sleep. Sometimes a neighbour, Mrs Allen, took my mother for treatment and to the post office to collect her pension. But if Mom had had words with Mrs Allen and they were not on speaking terms, these jobs fell on me again.

I hated those long hours sitting on hard wooden benches being shuffled from one queue to another, until after an interminable wait you heard you name being called and it was your turn to see the doctor. But much worse were the disdainful looks at school next day from the girls in my class. Any class with an absentee had a black mark against it in the register.

At the end of the term the class with most black marks was presented with a wooden spoon, which had to be carried by one girl for the length of the hall with the class in file behind her. The rest of the girls had a wonderful time, laughing fit to burst. It was all so jolly. Even the teachers were human and they laughed too. Jollity was not normally allowed, but this was the end of term so they all had a good time laughing at the little soul responsible for this spectacle, the one who had given them this chance for a break from lessons.

Everyone knew the culprit, the one who was absent the most, and I knew it too. I used to feel so dreadful walking in that procession and tried not to look up, hoping I could not be seen. There was some humanity among the staff because I never had to carry the spoon. Nor was I ever caned for absences.

At the start of a school year you were put into a new class, either going up a year or staying put. When my face appeared round the curtain to take my seat in the new class, the other girls would groan. 'Oh no - not her, she's always away.' The person who invented this system had a warped sense of humour and not an ounce of compassion.

Saint Barnabas's church and school
Photo: Mac Joseph

Father and Tommy

This period of my life is so very clear. Loosing my father was bad enough, but loosing my little brother Tommy a short time later etched those events on my memory so that I can't ever forget them. They marked a painful and permanent change to my life. I had been father's favourite, or was led to believe so, because I was very small and sickly and needed extra care for the first few months of my life. After his death and for the next ten years I was a little drudge. I was certainly not my mother's favourite, and during one of her rages she told me I should have been 'in the cut,' not Tommy.

In February 1924 my father, mother and little sister Florrie all fell very sick with pneumonia. They were quite helpless and could do nothing but lie in bed. I was only 6. When someone was ill in those days the neighbours rallied round. Mrs Edgington kept a second hand clothes shop on the corner of Sheepcote Street and Essington Street, and I remember her nursing Florrie on her lap in front of the bedroom fire. She made oatmeal gruel for my mother and I can smell it still. All sick people were fed on gruel because it was easy to digest and kept up the patient's strength.

With all the family sleeping in the one bedroom, parents and baby in the big bed, my brother and I in a smaller one, it was not possible for the neighbours to nurse all three patients. My father had to go to Dudley Road Hospital.

That was an awful day, sleeting and very cold. He had been taken from his bed, dressed and made to walk his last steps down the yard to the ambulance parked in the street. I walked alongside, crying, and wanted to go with him. Father had a blanket wrapped around him which was held in place by an attendant. The inside of that ambulance was bare as an empty box, the doors were closed and the only person who really loved me was driven away. Father died on the 8th March, a week after Florrie's first birthday.

There were no Funeral Parlours or Chapels of Rest for the poor, the dead were brought home where the undertaker measured the body for a coffin. The rooms where they lay had to be kept as cold as possible, with curtains drawn to shut out the sun.

My father lay downstairs, his coffin resting on trestles. My mother and sister had not recovered from their illness and were still in bed. I remember helping Mother downstairs to look at Father in his coffin. Death had its own feeling, like being in another world and shut out. It was a feeling of total emptiness and rejection, where you had to go about silently and speak in whispers in case you disturbed the dead.

Had Father got better things would still have been very bleak. He had no trade because twenty one years of his life had been spent in the Army. After discharge the only work he could get was as a porter, taking whatever it happened to be on a little truck to its destination. His last job was in The Priory, which ran from Steelhouse Lane to Old Square. When he was taken to hospital Mother had gone to his employer and asked them to keep his job open because he would not be away for very long. She was told that it was not possible as they needed someone right away. If ever there was a bleak house it was 3/5 Sheepcote Street, and as if my father's death were not enough, a greater tragedy was to follow six months later.

Tommy and I went to our father's funeral, Mother was too ill. Tommy wore a black suit and a high, white stiff collar. I was also in black with a stiff little hat of satin. It rested just short of my eyes so that only my ears kept it from covering my face. Next day I wore it to school and one little girl accused me of wearing my mother's hat.

It was a long journey to Witton Cemetery, and on the way back the hearse was stopped and the driver and bearers went into a pub. I had cramp in my legs from dangling them over those hard horsehair seats for a couple of hours.

It was, and still is, the custom to have food and drink for the mourners when they return from a funeral, and sometimes these occasions turn into a lively party. What a send off; but the truth is, you have to let them go. The sun rises and the moon sets with or without them and life starts again next day.

There was no food or drink at our house after Father's funeral and our larder would too often be empty. The bread winner, the provider of more than food, the rock on which my life had been built, was taken from away and I had to stand on my own.

Tommy went missing on 1st September that year. Lights from the neighbours' windows shone in the darkness. Normally the

12

shutters would have been closed with the only light from a
gas lamp on a wall bracket. From Edgington's step where I was
sitting I could see up our yard, I could see Broad Street to the
right and far down Sheepcote Street to my left until it vanished
into the night. Little groups of people walked up and down the
street, then someone would shout 'Tommy' and listen for an
answer. Suddenly, on the still, cold air came the piercing
whistle of a steam train from the railway yard at the bottom
of our street. To this day I hate to hear that sound, it
transports me back to that dreadful night.

My mother did not go to bed but walked the streets looking for
Tommy. She went to Ladywood Police Station to report him
missing. The constable on duty told her to go home, they would
start looking for him in the morning if he had not returned. He
would bet the little lad was asleep in some shop doorway and
would make his way home when it was light. My mother told
the policeman he was wrong, because Tommy was afraid of the
dark and would not stay out at night. She said she knew where
he was, he was in the cut, and why did they not do something
to get him out?

Mother walked all along the canal towpath and up each side of
Nile Street which lead down to it. Hour after hour she walked
and would not go home. She said he was in the water, she knew
he was. How could she have known? No one had reported seeing
him down 'the Nile'.

All the children we normally played and fought with were sound
asleep in their beds. The long, four week summer holiday had just
ended and school had started the previous day, Monday, so it was
early to bed from now on. The Morris's lived two doors from
Edgington's shop in Sheepcote Street, and the boys were Bobby,
Jackie and Harry, all between 6 and 10 years old. Their father
was very strict, so they would certainly have to obey the rules.

Then there was Jimmy Allen who lived in our yard. He was 10.
He did not say he had seen Tommy either. You would expect
children of their ages to have reported something so dreadful
as a small child falling into a canal.

Mr Morris eventually got the story out of his boys, about how
Tommy had followed them down to the canal with a slice of
bread and lard in his hand. There had been a bit of rough play.
Tommy had been hit on the head by a stone, thrown by no
one knew whom, and had fallen into the water.

If only those children could have known the heartache they caused in our house and to two lives, my mother's and mine. Have they regretted running, leaving a little boy aged 5 years and 10 months to sink into that black water and lie on the muddy bottom until his tiny body was dragged free.

The police used grappling irons to no effect for two days. Many of the boats used on canals were pulled by horses, but during the dragging operations a Cadbury's boat with a diesel engine turned up. The boatman in charge was stopped and then asked to start up his propeller again so as to disturb whatever was on the bottom of the canal. This was done and Tommy was found on 2nd or 3rd September 1924.

My mother forced her way through the crowd of women who had been watching the dragging, much to the disgust of the police. She threw herself down and tossed aside the sack which covered Tommy's small body. A policeman lifted her from the sodden mass that had been her beautiful little son. Our pictures of Tommy show his head covered in almost white curls, with big blue eyes and a sturdy little body. He was never ailing, like me. The policeman cleared a path through the crowd and more or less carried my mother from the towpath to a hole in the railings. Once she had been taken home he turned to the crowd of women and gave them a dressing down for allowing my mother to get to the towpath. He told them to get back to their homes asking, 'Did they call themselves women, enjoying seeing the agony of a mother?'

Someone had made that hole in the fence to make a short cut to work, so allowing children access to the canal and defeating its purpose. No child could have bent those bars.

Tommy lay in his coffin on a table beneath the opened bedroom window and my mother's bed was beside it, so she could not get any nearer to him. For a few days we all shared the same bedroom. In the mornings we would lift the cover from Tommy's face and just look at him, until one morning I said, 'Something's happened to him,' I told my mother. What it was I have never known. Mr Blakemore the local undertaker came from his shop in Bishopsgate Street to screw down the lid of the coffin and shut Tommy out of this world.

So many people came in sympathy to see us. His teacher, Mrs Robbins, kissed my mother on both cheeks, one kiss for Mom and the other for Tommy. She was a widow, there were plenty around after the war, and had also lost a son. For a brief time two grieving souls whose lives were worlds apart shared a common love, a mother's and a widow's.

There were masses of flowers with a basketfull hanging from both lamps of the hearse, which was drawn by two horses. It was followed by a horse drawn coach carrying mourners. Mr Blakemore walked in front and led the cortege up Essington Street, turning right into Ledsam Street to pass St Barnabas's School and Church where the cortege stopped.

Our Grandmother had gone to St Barnabas's School for a while and I had taken myself there on my 5th birthday. When Florence reached school age she also went there. We were a local family and in those days everyone knew everyone else because we lived cheek by jowl. Tragedy brings people closer together. When I think back to Tommy's funeral I see the hearse covered with flowers and hundreds of people lining the route to his school.

We left the flowers and the two baskets on the grave, but when we went back a few days later only one was left. Mother was so upset that she brought it home and hung it in our window.

My memories of this dreadful time end there. If only they could be wiped from my mind, like a chalk mark from a slate. As I grew older I came to understand the terrible blows fate dealt my mother in just six months, and my heart has softened towards her for the cruelty she poured on me. A few years ago I forgave her, I could not call myself a Christian until I had done that.

The Vicar from St Barnabas's, Mr Dugmore, came to console my mother. She was not a religious person and preferred her hymn books with handles. He told her that everything God did was for the best, and was quickly shown the door.

There was someone who held her hand and sympathised and brought a little consolation, someone from another world though she lived only half an hour's walk away. She lived in a big house in Edgbaston, had servants and a gardener or two, and her husband was a very prominent politician, yet she came up our yard to that little terrace house to bring Christian love to a poor, grief stricken soul.

Make no mistake, the last four words are not there to create effect. They describe my mother then, in 1924, and until her release when she died in 1934. I have seen her sink to her knees, tears streaming down her face, head raised, hands

clenched together, arms upstretched, begging God to tell her
what she had done that He had punished her so?

I would have loved to have met Mrs Neville Chamberlain, but I
was at school when she visited our house. She asked my mother
to go to her house on Saturday morning because she had something
for her. Westbourne Road was not far away and we were used to
walking. If we went anywhere, that was how we got there.

We walked over the crunchy gravel to the front door of Westbourne. A maid opened it and showed us into a hall, then left us
long enough for me to take notice of my surroundings. There was
probably more furniture in that hall than we had between the three
of us in our house. There were plants, tall plants which seemed to
be growing from the floor. When you are only three and a half feet
high everything above eye level dwarfs you, and I was overawed by
Mrs Chamberlain's house. The hall in which we sat opened up into
a wider room which could have been the inner hall leading to the
living rooms and staircase. Above this hallway I could see a corridor with doors along its length. Suddenly, one of them opened
and a man came out, looked at us sitting there, then went from
view. Was it the future Prime Minister who would meet Hitler
in 1938 and bring back his 'piece of paper'.

We were given more flowers for Tommy's grave, a small parcel
and a large envelope. My mother could not wait to get home to
open the package so we unwrapped it in the road. It contained
a tin of what was known then as patent food, which might have
been Ovaltine, Bournvita or Horlicks. These products were very
expensive so they never found their way to our pantry.

Mrs Chamberlain's envelope contained two sheets of printed
paper. On one was a signed message of sympathy dated 13th
September 1924, on the other a poem entitled Look Up. It
was always kept in the box with the other documents, such
as the rent book and insurance policies

WESTBOURNE,
EDGBASTON, BIRMINGHAM.

Sept 13 1924.

Dear Mrs Smith

THIS Poem goes to you with my best wishes and the hope that the words may help to comfort you in your great sorrow.

Believe me,

Yours very truly,

Annie Chamberlain

(Mrs. Neville Chamberlain).

Look Up!

LOOK up! He is not dead,
The loved one that ye weep.
Oh, lift that grief-bowed head;
He taketh rest in sleep.
Nay, nay! He is not dead.—
Look up!

Look up! He is not dead.
Often thy play-tired son
Crept to his little bed.
Before thy day was done.
He slept; he was not dead.—
Look up!

Look up! He is not dead.
His brief brave day's work o'er
Ere yet thy day has sped.
He sleeps, as oft of yore.
Why weep? He is not dead.—
Look up!

Look up! He is not dead.
One day thou too shalt rest,
And welcomes sweet be said.
When thou with him art blest.
Then wait; he is not dead—
Look up!

Look up! Love is not dead.
Love tender, patient, wise,
On him and thee doth shed
Its peace. Then lift thine eyes
Where Death itself is dead—
Look up!

T. Brunton Peatlie.

17

Mother and Me

I was about 7 when father died, the singing stopped and the beatings began. Our neighbours always spoke kindly of him and his love, not only for me but for all his children. When he was alive Mother's fiery temper did not reach the pitch it did later. At times it was uncontrollable and she would rave and curse, all the time punching me.

My mother had been a very pretty girl with dark curly hair and lovely teeth. I know this because whenever we met any of her former friends, their remark was always the same. 'Well Nellie, you've lost your good looks.' That remark was always answered with, 'I've had too many bleeding babbies.'

Too many children were indeed the cause of Mother's poor health, added to a poor diet. We never had enough money to buy nourishing food. Added to her poor health, fading eye sight and head pains caused by neuritis, was my father's death.

He had been the provider and just as important, the protector. A family needs a leader, someone to go to in times of stress or sickness, someone who understands you and who will listen. It can often help to unburden your worries and fears. The protector may not have a solution to your problem, but it can be very reassuring to know that someone cares enough to listen.

My mother could be very funny if she was in the right mood. She had grown up in the Horsefair district near the Hippodrome Theatre and had seen all the popular artists of the time. There was Florrie Ford, Vesta Tilley, Vesta Victoria, Nellie Wallace and Gerty Gitana. Then there was a man whose act involved dancing on the toes of his very long shoes whose name was Little Tich. My mother knew all the Music Hall songs so I grew up singing them too. Bill Bailey, Rag Time Cowboy Joe, Swannee.

This was Mother's good side, but at other times she was a nasty, quick tempered person. I would know as soon as I entered the house how I had to act. When she was in a bad mood her mouth clamped shut and she would grind her teeth with a menacing look. Lord help the one who caused her to boil over.

On one strange occasion we were going out to sit by the
Hall of Memory. The seats in that colonnade were sometimes
a blessing. It meant that my mother would find someone to talk
to and leave me free to play with my ball. We left the house
and had to walk past a group of people chatting at the end of
the entry. Someone said 'Hello' and that they thought it might
rain. Back came a reply I had never heard before and have not
heard since. 'It is better for the Lord to reign, than whores and
rogues'. Only 'whores' came out as whorers. We made our way
past them, leaving a puzzled little group.

On another occasion my mother was with some friends, a Mr
and Mrs Parry, at someone's house in St. Vincent Street. Everything was apparently going fine when trouble flared and our Mom
was in the middle of it. Someone told me that a row was going on
there so I ran round just in time to see Harold Parry pushing my
mother out of the door. She had drunk too much and was shouting.
He told her to go home and take her bastards with her, meaning
Florrie and me.

As we walked the short distance home everybody looked at us.
I was supporting our Mom by holding her arm to guide her and
hoping she would not fall, while little Florrie followed. She used
to be terrified of our mother at the best of times, poor little girl.

After a few hours sleep on the sofa, Mother woke up. I waited,
needing to test the atmosphere. I didn't want to risk her ranting
and raving all over again, but I knew that what Mr Parry had
called us was not right. I didn't know why, but I had to tell her,
which I eventually did in the evening. She went to the box of
important papers and took out the marriage lines. Then I had
to lead her back to the house where the trouble had been.

Mother stood on the pavement waving her marriage lines and
shouting for all to hear that her children were not bastards, and
inviting all and sundry to come and see and read for themselves that she had been lawfully married before we were born.
What had been a very good friendship with the Parrys ended
that day.

This was a pity because Harold and Alice Parry were very kind
people, and kindness was scarce in Florrie's life and mine. The
Parrys were attached to Florrie and often had her to stay at their
house. On one occasion they took me to the Lickey Hills. What

a treat, up tree lined Bristol Road on a tram to a few hours sheer delight, running and gambolling on the hills. I picked berries which were growing among the grasses and ate them as I went. It was heaven, no noise, no one to badger me and no orders with a tanning at the end of the day. There was just quietly spoken Mr and Mrs Parry sitting watching a little girl being happy for the first time since her father died. I could not be happy with my mother, I was not allowed to be because I should not have been there without Tommy. So for a day my miserable existence was forgotten, and I never forgot the kindness of the people who made it possible.

Mother's quick temper and ready violence were my life. I could sometimes avoid it because of her bad eyesight but once I was not able to dodge or run away because I was in bed. I had been reading by the light of a candle, both 'wasting my time' by reading and 'wasting' the candle. There were voices downstairs and I wanted to know who the visitor was. I crept down a few stairs and lifted the corner of a piece of baize which was nailed over the door to keep out the draft from the attic so that I could just see into the living room. My mother was 'entertaining' a man.

The man was Mr Clark who lived in the next yard. We knew the family but I had never seen him in our house before. His wife had died shortly before we had gone to live in Sherborne Street, and I remember seeing her in an invalid chair being pushed by her elder daughter. They had four children. Joey was the oldest at home and there was an older sister but she did not live with her father and was probably married. Vera was about 10 and Ronnie only 2. He was a lovely child with blonde hair and blue eyes.

Ronnie spent a lot of time with my mother; she loved that little boy. Was she trying to replace Tommy? One night we had Ronnie to sleep, only he didn't, he cried to go home, so at midnight we had to take him back to his father. I can remember thinking that Florrie could have done with some of that love. And me? I had given up expecting anything. I knew Mother had no love or feelings for me, which is why I left home at the first chance.

I paid for my peeping with a severe thrashing. Mother's steps came up the stairs and the bedroom door banged against the bed. She had come in a fury, her language as she punched me was terrible. I had rolled myself in the bed clothes so she could not hit me directly but I felt those blows just the same. She was going to kill me. Whenever I was in trouble she was going to kill me, and many times I wished I was dead.

Uncle Tom

One night when we were all in bed, mother, Florrie and
me, I was reciting or singing in the glow of a farthing candle
[.01p]. Even if you bought your candle from Aunt Kate and
Uncle Ernie Norman's shop you paid full price. 'Skinny mare',
my mother called her, and he was 'Snotty pocket'. I saw no
reason for arguing, they were nicknames amply earned.

Suddenly my mother sat bolt upright and told me to hush. We
sat rigid in bed, I didn't know what I was listening for but my
mother put out the candle and told me not to speak. Then out
of the dark, getting nearer, was the sound of someone singing,
a man's voice and a beautiful voice. It carried on the quiet air
from the bottom of Sheepcote Street up to our yard near Broad
Street. 'It's our Tom. He's had a skinfull'. My mother could
tell because her brother only sang when drunk and always the
one song, 'County Down'. He had been drinking down at
'Goosies', a pub opposite Nile Street, and was now bent on
making trouble. Who would get it tonight, us or the Nolans?

The Nolans who lived in Essington Street were Tom's inlaws,
but Tom and his wife Ada had parted and she and their son,
Dennis, lived with the Nolans. I remember them as very nice
people. Apart from Aunt Ada, her parents, a brother named
Micky and my cousin Dennis, there were two other sons who
lived elsewhere, one of whom was Frank.

Tom would go hop picking and then fruit picking as the seasons
went on, but there was no work in Worcester and Evesham in the
winter. This is when he came home to our Grandmother, and
every time he came he tormented his own family and his wife's.

My Grandmother's yard was opposite the Nolan's house, and before
Tom turned into it he would throw whatever came to hand through
the Nolan's window. Once he had knocked the oil lamp over; the
consequences could have been disastrous. But the Nolan's held the
Ace. Aunt Ada would go to court and summon him for not paying
maintenance.

Uncle Tom had just delivered his calling card through the Nolan's
window, when out sprang Frank and his brother. Tom took to his
heels and ran up our yard and into the brew house where he hid
among the washing tubs. Street lighting at this time was very

poor, with patches of almost pitch dark between lamp posts. Frank and his brother had lost sight of him but knew he had not got far, and they knew my mother was Tom's sister.

I remember seeing my Uncle Tom with his head in bandages and a Billy Cock hat perched on top. He had had a real beating. It was only whispered who was responsible and the knife was never found, but there was a grating in the middle of the Rec with water at the bottom. You would have thought after this that Tom would have gone away for good, but not Tommy Harkinson. As autumn came back so did he, and this time to our house. One down, two up, not much of a place and very little in it.

What drove Uncle Tom to break into our house that cold autumn night and destroy much of our belongings? The table lamp and the vases from the shelf were smashed, the clothes airing on the fire guard were thrown onto the grate, and all the time he was ranting.

When Mother knew he was paying us a call we left our beds and went up into the attic, I remember that night well. After he had left my sister was wrapped up in a shawl and we went out into the night up to Broad Street, looking for a policeman. I was crying and so frightened and cold. There had not been time to get dressed and I had no shoes on. I think Mother had wanted the police to see just what destruction he had caused and prosecute him. We did not find a policeman but my mother decided to take out a summons against him.

Next morning we went to the Law Courts in Corporation Street. I was filled with fear just entering the place. People seemed to be everywhere, and plenty of policemen. We were shown to a door guarded by a constable. He stopped us from going into the room saying that children were not allowed, but after explaining that my mother could not see to go by herself, I was let in.

We had to stand before a desk or table at which sat two upholders of the law, a man and a woman. My mother told her story of the happenings of the night before and wanted her brother, a half brother really from my Gran's second marriage, warned not to molest her anymore.

After listening to what she had to say, the hard faced man told her there was nothing they could do in the matter and said she was mostly to blame for encouraging him to the house when he was sober. This, of course, was only assumption. He could not know anything about us. Had he lived in our street or Essington St he would have made a very different assessment. After this episode one of our neighbours gave Mother a police whistle to summon help if ever Tom came back.

He never did visit us again, day or night, and faded from the scene for many years. I grew up in fear of him, but as I grew older this turned to anger anger and loathing. How could one human being treat another with such inhuman callousness? So many times I thought I would find him and get my revenge, not only for that episode, but for when he came round after Tommy's body was dragged from the canal.

My father had died only six months before but Uncle Tom had not come then to offer his sympathy; after Tommy's death he was almost blaming my poor, sick mother. Tom nagged on, asking what brought Tommy to the canal? Why had he been allowed to go? And on and on. My mother's cousin Jinnie had come to see us with Uncle Jim, who turned on Tom and silenced him.

Our Ted

After my father's death I became aware of another member of our family in Canada because I had to write to him at Mother's dictation. His name was Edward Endicott, always known as 'Our Ted', and his address was Farm, Callender, Ontario, Canada. The town later became famous as the birthplace of the Dianne quintuplets, the first to survive.

I used to be so proud of having a brother, especially one in Canada, and I used to brag to the other kids about what we were going to have when 'Our Ted' came home. Pianos were all the rage in the late 1920s and we were going to have one when 'Our Ted' returned. Where I got that idea I will never know. It was not as if Ted sent us presents. Christmases came and went but we never had anything from Canada, not even a card on birthdays. I am doing him an injustice. We once had a box of maple syrup candy.

I never questioned his surname. My mother's name was Smith, as was Tommy's, Florrie's and mine, But Mother's maiden name had been Endicott. Had I asked her why Ted's surname was the same as her unmarried name I would probably have received a belting and told not to be 'So bleeding cheeky.' Mother's stock answer to any question was 'Children should be seen but not heard.' This applied not only in our house but was the universal adult catch phrase. Beside it lay another pearl of wisdom, 'Speak when you're spoken to and not before'.

There were so many other questions I wanted answered. Why did Uncle Tom behave to us the way he did? Why did Gran not want me in her house, or rather, why didn't she want us? Florrie was only a little girl, a lovely little girl with blonde curls like Tommy's. Perhaps it was because I always wanted to help Gran, like the time I helped throw the coal down the cellar steps. The coalman had left quite a bit on the cellar head, so I thought I would be useful. The lump I picked up must have been big, because I failed to let it go and followed it down to the bottom. I remember crawling back up the steps crying my heart out. For that incident I was branded a pest. 'Keep her out, she's into everything.'

Not only did Gran not want us in her house, she once came up our yard drunk. We were in bed, early as usual because it saved burning coal or lamp oil. Gran started to 'carry on' very loudly so that all the neighbours could hear what she was shouting, and none of it was good. Then she ended a sentence with, 'You and your old man's gettings', meaning us children. At this, Mother lifted up the sash window, took the big jug of water from the table and threw the contents over Gran. She reeled from the shock, but went away and never repeated that performance.

My father was twenty years older than my mother, nearer my Gran's age. So for this Mother was vilified. What did they want of her? Undoubtedly in her younger days she had led a very wayward life. I had brothers and sisters who bore her maiden name, Ted being her first child and the rest dying as babies. Not knowing the facts I can't pass comment, except to say she always claimed that Ted's father was a man named George Swan. She may have kept me from speaking but could not stop me from listening. Minny Checkley who lived in our yard once told my mother that she had seen Swan, and what Mother called, and wished him, is unprintable. I learned the whole sorry story over the following years just by keeping my ears open and my mouth shut.

I learned how my Grandmother reacted when my mother told her she was going to have a baby. She beat her then threw her out of the house saying that she had, 'Made her bed, so must lie on it.' Mother was 18 years old.

To have a daughter who had got herself into trouble was such a disgrace. In those days people thought far more about what the neighbours would say than they do now, and what the neighbours thought about most things was uncharitable. The stigma of an unmarried pregnancy would follow a family for ever, and it was because of that one human failing that Mother's family did not want us. That and the fact that after my father died we were desperately poor. The family need not have worried. Mother would not have asked any one of them for a match.

My Canadian half brother's full name was Edward George Endicott and this was his story. As a small boy he lived with my mother in Sheepcote Street, up a yard which ran beside Baylis's tube factory. At the top of the yard were the dustbins, lavatories and the brew houses, where the washing was done. At the back of these and easily accessible were the offices of Baylis's. Ted smashed a window and broke into them to steal some stamps and money. How much money he took I never knew, but he spent it on bus rides.

For this Ted was to be put into a 'Home', which happened to be Father Hudson's at Coleshill. It was 1920, when Ted was 12 and I was 3 years old. Coleshill was then far beyond the eastern edge of the City because most of the suburbs east of Washwood Heath had not been built. For us it might as well have been on the other side of the world. My mother never visited Ted but my father did. Perhaps he went by train and walked the couple of miles from Water Orton station. I know he had to cross fields because on one occasion he was chased by a bull, so the story went. With money in short supply Ted did not have many visits because Father found it hard enough to keep his family on a porter's wage. I have often wondered whether he walked all the way to Coleshill.

On my father's last visit he was told that Ted had been moved, just like that. What a shock, to go all the way to Coleshill to be met with news that the child you had gone to see was no longer there. Not only did my father not see him that day, he never saw Ted again. A bigger shock was in store. Father asked where he had been sent, thinking that it would be a similar institution in the Midlands. Ted had been sent to Canada.

My mother was never informed nor consulted in any way. She was never asked to agree. No forms noting her approval were ever signed by Mother or any member of Ted's family. So there he was in Canada, ignorant of the facts which had taken him there but always blaming my mother.

My brother was not the only child to be sent to Canada from an orphanage, but he was not an orphan and neither were hundreds who were sent to Canada and Australia. Families were split up and many so called child migrants never saw their parents or brothers and sisters again. Most of the children in these homes were there because their father or mother had died or were too poor to keep them at home. Some, like Ted, had committed an offence against society and whatever it had been, were often given a life sentence. The poor in those days were like sitting ducks, we had no chance. We did not know who to complain to or how to do it and had no expectation of being treated with respect if we did. The fact had to be accepted, Ted had been sent to Canada and that was that.

Why were these children sent abroad? For a better life and to learn a trade, usually farming whether they wanted to be farmers or not. Imagine what it must have been like for a boy from a city, used to people around him, the hustle and bustle, noise and activity of people he knew, and worse, his friends all gone.

[Editor's Note. The terrible story of child migrants only became a scandal in the 1990s. One typically harrowing account of a little girl who was sent to Australia is *Flo, Child Migrant from Liverpool* by Flo Hickson (Plowright Press ISBN 0 951696 03). She was told the complete untruth that her parents had died.]

I have no memory of Ted before he went to Canada but I do remember his return. He was wearing a short coat patterned in bold red squares. What an impact it had. Clothes in those days were very sombre - black, brown and mud coloured for relief. When coloured films were invented you saw lumberjacks wearing similar jackets. He must have been wearing trousers, shoes, etc, but my memory is of a slight figure walking up the yard in that lovely jacket. He was then 18 years old and a stranger to Florrie and me.

There was no homecoming party because we had no relatives who would acknowledge us, though Gran, Aunt Kate and Uncle Ernie lived a stone's throw away. And there were no old friends to greet Ted, he just appeared. I don't think my mother knew when he was actually arriving. His letters from Canada had been few and far between and were never informative.

Whatever Ted learned in Canada, it was not farming, so he was without a trade. He could not have enjoyed the life out there because he made no effort to pursue it when he returned home.

Ted had a lot of adjusting to do. From the great open spaces he was back to grimy streets, smoke filled air and noise, with not a blade of grass to be seen. Our house must have seemed like a box, a very small box. Ted must have felt hemmed in after six years on a farm. Instead of cattle and sheep, he would see draught horses pulling carts full of goods from local factories, and he had come back to the source of so much unhappiness.

Ted also had to get to know his family after a gap of six years, a big part from anyone's life. He had gone away a child but to judge from some of the things he did, he had not grown up much. He soon discovered that his mother could still give him the length of her tongue and would have given him more had she been able to catch him.

My mother liked a drink and one night sent me with a bottle to fetch half a pint of ale from Mr Partridge's outdoor [off licence] on the corner of Oozell Street and Sheepcote Street. You can still get beer in this way from a few places, but then it was common to send a bottle or jug. When beer was sold to a child it had to be in a bottle with a label over the top to stop the child drinking it. I had many a taste, despite the label.

Coming back up the yard with the bottle I was met by Ted. He took the bottle and removed the label, then put it under the outside tap and filled it to the top with water. When I gave it to Mother she knew straight away that all was not as it should be. The weight of the bottle told her there was more liquid than she had paid for, but she could not see what was in it or how much until she put it to her lips to taste. She gave a great bellow and I ran out of the house as far away from her as I could to be out of range of that bottle.

Mother did not throw the bottle at Ted but he got plenty of verbal abuse. He was left in no doubts that if she wanted a drink she would bleeding well have one, and he needn't think he was running the place either. I stood rooted to the spot, petrified, knowing my mother and her temper and how long she could keep it flaming. She would not forgive or forget and would be in a foul mood for days.

Ted got his own back in a nasty sort of way. He would suddenly start singing, 'Swannee. How I Love You. How I Love You, My Dear Old Swannee', this of course was in reference to his father, George Swan. I was not supposed to know that he was taunting my mother but I would see her face go suddenly taut. She looked confused at these assaults but never took the bait. Perhaps it might have been better for us all if she had, and cleared the air.

Ted's return had not made life better for any of us. Our status was the same, poor, but there was more aggravation, and I was uncomfortable with a stranger about the place. We never saw my piano and I stopped talking to my friends about Our Ted.

One morning Ted went out and returned carrying a box which he opened to reveal what looked like small, loosely packed bundles of string. It got us guessing because I had never seen them before, but I could read from the packet that this was Shredded Wheat. This was living. Ted had got fed up, or rather tired of not being fed, so he decided to buy his own breakfast. In Canada he had been used to having Shredded Wheat. The world was beginning to reveal some of its mysteries to us, but it was years before I had Shredded Wheat again.

Even at 18 Ted was just a boy at heart, and a sly one at that. One afternoon I walked in on a row on between him and our mother. She was accusing him of drinking the milk, which he was denying. He was adamant, he had not drunk that milk and was being falsely blamed. When I walked in Ted turned to me and said, 'She's had it.' He really dropped a brick that time and I was elated, at last, it wasn't me. He had been away so long, that he did not know my likes or dislikes and was told not to tell, '.. bleeding lies because she don't like milk.', which I didn't.

On another occasion Ted gave me some money and told me to go to Mrs Giles' sweet shop for a block of Cadbury's Milk Chocolate. I had never seen such a big block of chocolate. I thought you could only buy one penny bars, or 'flakes' at three halfpence.

Ted was spending the money he had brought home from Canada, because he was not working. Nor do I remember any talk of him getting a job. There was a great deal of unemployment at this time after the First World War, and being so young with no trade or experience of any kind he did not have a chance. The ex-servicemen were always considered first but some of them were reduced to singing in the streets for coppers.

Ted spent a lot of time time at Gran's and Aunt Kate's and my
mother resented this. She was never slow to speak her mind on
any matter and this did upset her. She blamed them for enticing
Ted away from her, but you could not blame him for wanting
to get out of the house because there was no comfort in staying.
He was sleeping in the attic where there was just a bed but no
other furniture. If you leaned far enough out of the window on
a clear day you might catch a glimpse of a passing cloud, but
the sky was usually black with smoke from factory chimneys.
We were born to this environment and knew nothing different,
it seemed the normal way of things, so we just kept coughing
and hoped to live another day.

Living in an acrimonious atmosphere day after day had effects
on me. One day I met my cousin Katy, Aunt Kate's daughter,
on the school stairs, told her what I thought about her keeping
my brother away from his home and then pushed her. When Ted
heard about it he gave me such a telling off 'For pushing Katy
down the stairs.' She had not fallen down the stairs, but even
if she had, I would not have cared. I felt I had dealt a blow
for my mother. And so the seeds of acrimony were sown.

Ted's views were all one sided. He had not known Tommy
or the sorrow of his and my father's deaths in such a short
space of time. Our relatives had not rallied round to help,
the neighbours had. We had good neighbours who had looked
after us when the family was first taken ill, then after the two
deaths, and again when Mother had to go into the Eye Hospital.
In Ted's eyes though, his relatives were fine. He was always
made welcome at their homes and knew nothing of the slights
we had suffered, nor of my mother's struggles to look after
us with her failing eyesight and poor health.

I suppose Ted could see that things were pretty desperate; he
was experiencing poverty in its true sense. But instead of trying
to better our situation he took the easy way out and left us to it
by enlisting in the Dorset Regiment for seven years. They do say
the Army makes 'men'. I don't know about that but I do know
that Ted did not take kindly to the process, because after only a
month or two he wished he had not joined. He wrote to Uncle
Ernie asking for a loan of £100 to buy himself out, but he didn't
get it. Uncle Ernie was a businessman and I suppose he thought
Ted was not a very good investment, so he had to 'soldier' on
and make the best of it. He came home for one leave and was
then sent to India.

This was how I came to be writing letters and addressing envelopes to places in India. However, Ted was no more prolific at letter writing than he had been in Canada and if anything wrote far less, causing my mother to comment if ever his name was mentioned, 'He's forgotten us'.

Ted did not forget Aunt Kate and sent her a picture of himself with some silk to make herself something. Neighbours told my mother about the parcel but Mother never let on that she knew. This was one of the many indignities she had to suffer from Ted which made me so sorry for her, even though she abused me shamefully. I was the one who had to sit and watch her crying when we were alone, but if I did anything to annoy her I would be accused of 'Being as bad as him in India'.

My mother must have been desperate and at a very low ebb when she made me sit and write the begging letter to Ted, the first and last I ever wrote. It was a tremendous thing for her to do, to swallow her pride and be humble. What was it she so badly needed that she had to ask her son in India for help? She was not asking for anything for herself, not she, it was something for one of his sisters.

I would have started the letter with 'Dear Ted', and hoped he was well, etc. Then, 'Could you please send me two shillings to buy some shoes with?'

How can twelve words can stay in one's memory for over sixty years just as clearly as if I had written them sixty hours ago. We are told to forget the past, which is dead and gone, but if the past will not die you can't help but remember. I would prefer to forget this little episode of my childhood because it is so painful.

I must have been 'down on my uppers', a phrase often used in those days. Strictly, it meant the soles of your shoes were so worn away that the sides were rubbing on the ground. For us it was enough that the holes had grown too big to be covered by cardboard. A piece of cardboard would only last if the weather was fine, so you were really walking barefooted. If your feet were cut, wet or frozen, that was too bad. At the back of our school classroom was a free standing cast iron stove. One day when the hot lid had been taken off to let out more heat, Nellie Field trod on it and burnt her foot.

The letter to Ted would have taken two or three weeks to reach him, and Ted being busy soldiering would not have a lot of time to write a reply. There was once a gap of about eighteen months between his letters, which prompted my mother's remark 'He's forgot us'. I don't know how long it was before the postman brought the anxiously awaited letter from India. Eventually it arrived, bearing an Indian stamp in Annas. It was a pity Ted did answer, far better for his letter to have been lost in the post. Ted's reply was:

'You need all the shillings you can get in the King's Army.'
Also, this request, *'Can you send me a picture of my father?'*

Once again my mother had been humiliated but now Ted's spite had spilled over onto his sister. What would Ted have thought if I had replied that I knew we had different fathers but had no picture of his. My regret was that we hadn't a picture of our father, Florrie's and mine, either.

I wrote back saying, 'They do say I am like my father so when you look at my picture, you will be seeing him.' I don't remember sending him a picture of myself then, when I was about 12 years of age, but when I was 14 I sent one in which I was wearing my posh frock with a little lace cape over my shoulders.

Once more I had acted out the role of being innocent to Ted's innuendoes, and did so until our last meeting on this earth. I don't think he looked upon Florrie and me as his sisters, half or otherwise. Even so, I always looked upon him as a brother; the fact that we had different fathers did not come into it.

Ted had so many problems and a great big chip on his shoulder which he carried all his life. I know my mother was not the easiest person to be with but I do think he should have stayed and helped to raise us and keep us together as a family. His leaving home to join the Army made life much harder for Florrie and me because Mother became more bitter and took out her spite on us.

Gran

Gran was my mother's mother. Her mother was Betsy (Elizabeth) Carroll and she and her husband, Patrick, had come from County Clare in Ireland.

Gran had been married twice. Her first husband was Edward Endicott but he had died at the age of 30, leaving Gran with three young children. There was a boy named for his father, a daughter named Clara after her mother and Nellie, my mother. Before they married my Grandfather had said that he would like to have three children, 'Two to fight and one to see fair play.' He had his wish but did not live to raise and enjoy them, dying when my mother was 2 years old.

The day Grandad was taken to hospital Gran rode with him in the ambulance to Dudley Road Hospital. As they entered, with the wheels rattling over the cobble stones, Grandad looked at Gran and said, *'Over the stones, Rattle the bones, Here comes the poor pauper, Nobody owns'*.

Whether he already knew these words or was prompted to say them by the circumstances, we will never know. He died soon after. Gran told me that as his coffin was being lowered into the grave, she had the feeling of something inside her turning to ice, a feeling that never left her.

The Endicott family came to the rescue by taking the second child, Clara, to live with them. She was 4 or 5 years old. Gran saw very little of her child for some years, but one Saturday afternoon at the Rag Market she saw Clara among a crowd of bargain hunters. She described to me how lovely she looked, 'in a skirt and a nice blouse.' I asked Gran, 'Did you speak to her?' She said she that couldn't, she didn't like to, which shows how far they had drifted apart.

At the time Gran was telling me this she was in her 80s, so until her death at the age of 82 plus, she never knew what happened to Clara. On that Saturday Clara had been a 'face in the crowd', a memory to cherish, perhaps to cry over.

Being left with two children to bring up in the 1890s must have been a struggle. The Homer family employed Gran at their home as a cleaner. They were well known among the market traders and were among the few and elite florists who traded in the Market Hall at the old Bull Ring.

Gran would have had other work because the money from one job would not have been enough to keep them. No doubt she washed clothes for other households in their own homes or collected it for washing and ironing at her house. It was money hard earned and often at the cost of paying a child minder.

However, things were not going right. Whether Gran herself decided it was the right thing to do or the authorities gave her no choice, her son, Ted, was sent to Middlemore's Homes somewhere in Birmingham. Later he became yet another child who was sent to Canada.

Gran once told me how she had tried to get him back and was carrying him home hidden under her shawl. A policeman stopped her and asked what she was carrying. When he saw the child he said, 'Take him back', but in a kindly way. Gran did not elaborate on these incidents, they were just snippets of events told as they came to her mind.

Gran later married a man called Harkinson-Thomas and had two sons and two daughters. His nickname was 'Dead En, but how he came by it I have no idea. He worked in a brass foundry somewhere in Birmingham, a dirty, unhealthy job in badly ventilated buildings.

Whether he retired from this job or had to leave because of his health, I can't say, but money had to be got somehow to keep the family. Despite his nickname, Dead En had initiative. He embarked on an outdoor career collecting unwanted clothing in a cart. This took him to healthier and more salubrious parts of town such as Edgbaston and Harborne, where the pickings were best.

He had no overheads because there were no dues or rates to pay, he was his own gaffer and his time was his own. Even so, you had to call at the big houses regularly or your face would soon be forgotten and somebody else could pinch your houses. When the little maid answered the door you would ask humbly, 'Is there anything for me today, please?'. She would say, 'I will go and ask my mistress' and float off into the comfortable interior. Humility was expected, and where your bread and butter was concerned it was as well to be thrice humble.

At times there would be some decent things in Dead En's cart, though he walked miles to get them. A blouse or a skirt might fetch a few coppers from someone who was looking for a bargain, and that was enough to pay for a loaf of bread and a bit of cheese

To prop up his clothing empire Dead En needed a winter side-line for when the weather kept him indoors. Being now a business man, and with a bit of pushing from Gran - 'We've got nothing for dinner,' he stirred himself to action and threw all his energy and resources into the timber business. He was short in both and no chicken, but he bought an orange box and was in business. With fires the only source of heating and cooking, a bundle of wood was always handy. The problem was that there were so many other woodsellers.

One day the rent man called at an inopportune moment and at the wrong door, choosing to walk down the entry leading to the kitchen. This was where the firewood was chopped and bundled. There was nothing in that room, so if a piece of the wood flew into the air nobody had to duck. It was a perfect wood chopper's room until the rent man walked in and saw the chopper in Dead En's hand. It was probably less the use of a dwelling house for business than the shattered quarry tiles in the floor that upset him. Strict orders were given to the effect that no more chopping of wood should be done in that room again, and a block must be used forthwith.

The rag trade and firewood businesses went on so long as Dead En was able. Then he took to his bed and could do nothing for four years. The only time I remember seeing him was at Gran's house in Essington Street. As I closed the door and looked around I saw a hunched figure on a chair by the fireplace with a blanket round his shoulders. He did not look up or speak to me, but my gaze was riveted on his feet which were badly neglected. His toenails were so long they had grown up and over his toes. Gran got out of bed one morning saying she would soon get the fire going and bring him a cup of tea. En did not answer, he had died during the night while Gran slept on.

I remember Dead En lying on the bed covered completely by a white sheet. On each side was a big white candle because he was a Roman Catholic.

Just after Dead En's death Gran had a visitor who asked after him. Hearing that he had died, he offered 'sincerest condol-ences', put on his hat and turned to leave. Gran thought she

might as well ask why he wanted to see En. It was a little
matter of a suit he had bought on credit, and for which no
payments had been made. But, of course, the visitor said, he
understood the situation and the matter was closed. With the
corner of her apron covering her face as she closed the door,
the caller would have thought Gran was upset about her dearly
beloved, so recently departed. Actually she was trying to stifle
her laughter. Poor Dead En had never owned a suit in his life.
Gran thought it must have been their son who had the same
name as his father and had given his their address as his own.
I'm glad you found something to laugh about that day, Gran.
It must have been your first good laugh for many a year.

Lodgers and Neighbours

With Ted gone his room became available for letting, and I can
remember two lots of lodgers who lived there.

There was a young couple called Alice and Ernie Miles, I think
they were newlyweds. Years later I saw Ernie from a moving
bus as he stood outside The Bull public house in Stetchford. I
would have liked to ask him if he remembered when he lived
with us, and the occasion when I was washing my hair in a
bowl of water on the table. With lather all over my head and
in my eyes, I couldn't see the fire or the full kettle of rinsing
water sitting on it, so I asked Ernie to pour its contents over
my head. He obliged but didn't test the heat of the water.
It must have been near boiling and I let out such a scream.
All he said was, 'You did tell me to pour it over you.'

The other lodgers were a family named Chatwin, mother, father,
a little boy and a girl. They were small people but so pleasant,
always smiling. I can't think why because they had no permanent home and no possessions to speak of.

Once while they were out I crept up the stairs and pushed open
the attic door. They had nothing, there was no stick of furniture
in the room, just a heap of something in the corner which might
have been clothes or covers to keep them warm at night. So the
Chatwins had just a roof over their heads when they lay down to
sleep on those bare attic boards. That family stayed in my mind.
We were poor by anybody's standard but these people had even
less, yet they could smile.

They would go to the wholesale markets in Jamaica Row
at the end of the day and sort among the discarded fruit and
vegetables. I suppose what they did not eat themselves would
fetch a copper or two from someone glad to have a bargain.

A good dinner could be made from a 9 penny rabbit [3.75p]
and a few vegetables. What you asked for was a pound of
'mixed', which consisted of a carrot, an onion and a parsnip.
To these you added a spoonful or two of pearl barley to make
a feast for less than a shilling [5p]. Only you didn't pay 9
pence for a rabbit from Mr & Mrs Chatwin, you got one
for 6 pence.

I had to learn how to skin a rabbit, which was not an easy job
for a child. You got your education the hard and practical way.
Later in life I met a newly married woman who thought she
would impress her husband with a rabbit pie when he returned
from work. She was crying when her husband arrived home to
no dinner, having spent hours trying to pluck it.

A tragedy happened in the attic while the Allens, or Sabins,
were living with us. She was Mrs Allen, he was Mr Sabin. I
don't remember anything about it except that the victim was
named Nellie, like me, and about my age. She must have been
playing with the grate and set her clothes on fire. My father
heard the child's screams, ran up the stairs and wrapped his
coat around her. When he brought her down the neighbours
crowded around the door. Les Crutchly from three doors away
took Nellie from my father, ran to the tap just yards from our
door and held her under the running water. It was no use and
she died in hospital a few days later. Fifteen years later this
family were living in Lichfield Rd, Aston and lost another
little girl in similar circumstances.

Having lodgers was a small source of income which helped to pay
our weekly rent of 4 shillings and 8 pence [23p]. I suppose you
would get 2 shillings for an attic [10p]. Of course, you had to be
careful about taking lodgers. If the Board of Guardians found out
the 2 shillings would be deducted from your 'Parish money'.

The lodgers could reach the attic only through your living room,
so there would be comings and goings up and down the stairs all
day long. They had to come down for the least thing, to get water
from the tap in the yard and go to the lavatory, so you lost your
privacy along with the other inconveniences. Our lodgers never
stayed long, just long enough to help my mother to get a few
extra shillings.

Outside your own house with possible lodgers, were the neighbours. The community was a strange mixture. On the one hand there was dependence and need met with generous kindness, and on the other, loud, brawling arguments and permanent feuds. What we all had in common was awful poverty in an world ruled by a haughty and moralising authority, which seemed to look benignly at whatever landlords and employers chose to do.

I heard some heartbreaking stories. Neighbours might quarrel about nothing at all, but often over their children's disputes. Mothers would rush to defend their own children and it would erupt into a nasty brawl. There would be lots of shouting and threats, such as 'I'll report you to the Parish' about such and such a thing. When these threats were carried out a Parish visitor arrived to investigate the claim that someone was making money and not telling the authorities. If found guilty the family would lose their allowance, and from that there was no appeal.

Sometimes words slung about were too offensive to be ignored, so someone had to be 'summoned', that is, taken to court. This happened between Mrs Thacker and Mrs Goode. The process started with the complainant stating her case to a presiding magistrate who then would decide whether there were grounds to issue a summons. Mrs Thacker complained of verbal abuse which included being called a cow. The magistrate looked up, adjusted his spectacles to regain his composure and gave his verdict. 'Then you should feel flattered, the cow is a clean animal, so go home.' He could have added, 'And live in peace'. Case dismissed and a waste of half a crown [2 shillings and 6 pence - 15p]

My mother and Mrs Goode were not good friends and on one occasion they came to blows in the yard. What a commotion, with us kids screaming and crying and trying to part them. I need not have worried about our Mom, she would have been the victor. She was a hard nut and it would have taken more than one Mrs Goode to have got the better of her. The only thing that calmed my mother was eventual poor health and blindness.

Mrs Thacker and her family lived next door to us at Number 4. She had lost her leg as a child when knocked down by a horse tram in Hurst Street and walked with a crutch. She was also a widow, which explained why three of her four children were in homes. A son, Albert, and a daughter of about my age were in Monyhull Institution. I only saw Albert and his sister once, but I remember her crying when she was due to go back to the home. The other son, Charlie, was in the Blue Coat School which then looked onto St Philip's churchyard from where the Prudential building now stands. From there Charlie could could walk to Sheepcote Street in ten minutes, so he did come home to visit.

Mrs Thacker's other daughter, Ada, lived at home and had a little boy named Dennis. He used to mess his trousers, so his company was not sort after. Ada also had a baby called Hetty, but she died and I was one of the bearers at her funeral.

A child taken into the Blue Coat School would have been an orphan or with just one living parent. Charlie Thacker had only his mother, as did another local boy at the school, Billy Pummel. There was also a girl from a yard just above the Rec in Essington Street whose mother was a widow.

The Blue Coat boys wore a uniform which could have come from a Charles Dickens novel. There were tail coats sporting a mass of shiny brass buttons, a white stock around the neck, a tam o shanter, knee breeches, long knitted socks and black boots. The girls wore cloaks over their skirts with large hats and looked comparatively subdued.

Charlie Thacker, I thought, was a bit stuck up and never played with the rest of us yard children. Perhaps what put him off was the occasion I had been told to empty the pow, or chamber pot. Charlie was standing on his front doorstep and our doors were only separated by the thickness of one brick. I suppose dashing out with the pow in one hand, having used the other to open the door, I was a bit off balance.

I can still see the disgust on Charlie's face and hear him calling me a 'dirty, filthy thing'. Even so, I was laughing as I ran back indoors to tell my mother what had happened. Usually there was just pee in the pot, but if a child wanted to do a No. 2, no one was getting up in the dark, cold night to take it to the lavatory. I give the credit, or blame, on this occasion to Florrie.

Charlie Thacker was not one of us, you see. He was somehow apart and aloof. What none of us knew or ever gave a thought to was that he was having a good education and regular meals in an organised, disciplined environment. He was away from his mother and family, and perhaps life was harsh in the Blue Coat School, but I'm sure Charlie did not end up in a factory, scratching for a living which was all most of us had to look forward to. I must say he wore his uniform well and, I think, proudly too.

Mrs Thacker used to do 'out work', such as polishing small articles, or mounting buttons and pins on display cards. Later this practice was referred to as pin money, usually by house-wives who found it hard to manage on their husband's wages but were too proud to admit it. They were exploited by their employers and worked long hours for a pittance. Many of the laws passed to protect these workers seem to be ineffective or are ignored because such practices still go on. But at least today we have various state benefits to fall back on, while the Mrs Thackers of the 1920s had nothing between the pins and the Parish.

I can remember her sitting at a window with the net curtain pulled back to give more light. With head bent and a pair of wire framed spectacles on the end of her nose, she rubbed away madly at some article, too busy to see me watching. She used a tool very like a miniature golf club which every so often she would dip into a little container. She went on burnishing until you could see the article shine like the sun.

She had various objects to work on. At one time she was doing silver or silver plated cruets stands which stood on a base supp-orted by little feet and were lifted up by a ring. The number of containers (pepper, salt etc) determined their shape and size, so those holding a mustard pot and vinegar bottle were the largest. Today they fetch good prices as antiques. All Mrs Thacker knew about them was the stands. She never saw the complete assembly unless she went window gazing at the jewellers' shops in Corporation Street,

Sometimes Mrs Thacker worked on silver or plated shells which fitted on the palm of her hand. I used to love those. They were used to hold pats of butter, a fact I learned when I went into domestic service at Upwood in Barnt Green.

There were also buttons to be sewn onto cards printed with the maker's name and mark. They held six buttons or twelve which had to be regularly spaced and sewn in a particular way.

This was a long and tiring job, but I think the worst job of all was the pins. You were given a strip of pink paper folded vertically, concertina fashion, into which thousands of pins had to be fitted, straight and even. I remember helping someone to do this job, but only once. Have you ever had a pin down your nail?

The Goodes lived next door to the Thackers. Ernie and Rosie Goode went to Severn Street School which was quite a long way off, but it was one of the very few schools offering free dinners to the very poor children. So Ernie and Rosie had a school dinner, but no breakfast or tea. Late in the afternoon they would stand at the entrance to our yard. If the workmen passing on their way home had eaten all their lunch and could not pass on the odd sandwich, the Goodes would certainly go to bed hungry. Begging is such a harsh and condemning word.

There had once been a man in the Goode household, always known as 'dad', but he had died. He name was Willetts and I remember him as tall, very thin and balding, with spectacles. If a man and woman lived together unmarried the man's death gave the woman no claim to the widow's pension, which only came into force in 1925. So the woman and children were left in a pitiful state. Work was hard to come by in the years just after World War I. Mrs Goode worked as a cleaner at the Childdrens' Hospital for a pittance. When she was not working she sent Ernie and Rosie to ask the passing workers for left over food. They didn't actually hold out a begging bowl but just hoped they would be lucky enough to eat that night.

The Goodes had another idea. If an empty orange box came their way it would be broken up and made into bundles tied with string. They were piled into an old pram and pushed around the streets to sell at 1 penny a bundle[.4p]. If another hawker of firewood had knocked on the same door before them offering, say, two bundles for 1 penny, it was hard luck and meant more walking and knocking on doors for Rosie and Ernie. If they met the competition there would be a row about territorial rights. If luck was with them they went home with a few coppers to start the next day.

Mrs Good had an older daughter called Prudence but she was not around the yard very much, spending a lot of time with her friend, Ella Dudley. Ella lived in Broad Street at the back of Miss Lee's sweet shop, which was directly opposite Sheepcote Street. Ella and Pruie wore their long hair down

their backs tied with a bow. The 'top of the pops' at this
time was a song, 'My girl's got long hair, got long ginger
hair'. They don't write songs like that any more. Us kids
would walk up the street behind the two of them singing
this ditty until they got fed up and told us to clear off.

The hairstyle just described was worn by the filmstar Mary
Pickford, so Ella and Pruie lived their fantasy life, Mary
Pickfords for a few hours each day. This style was super-
ceded by the 'bob'. I remember coming home from school
one day to find that my mother had had her hair 'bobbed'.
I was upset about it because combing my mother's long
curly hair was to me a pleasure. But as she used to say,
'You might just as well be out of this world as out of
the fashion'.

The Recreation Ground on the corner of Essington Street
and Sheepcote Street was the place for the neighbours and kids
to meet and play. This was where you let off steam, made new
friends or fell out with old ones, vowing that you would never
play with them again, until the next day. The Rec was also near
enough for me to hear Mother calling if she wanted me to run
an errand. That was often, so I never dared go far from home.

I was playing there one day when my mother and Mrs Thacker
appeared, only she was not Mrs Thacker when out of earshot,
but Mrs Nacker, a dreadful word in those days. Mrs Thacker
lurched along on her crutch and when they came up to the swings,
my mother somehow got her to sit on one. She then took the poor
woman's crutch away and pushed the swing as high as she dared.
The old lady was screaming and laughing and holding on for grim
death. The park keeper and all the kids in the Rec came to join
in the fun. When my mother finally helped her off, Mrs Thacker's
face was wet with tears, she had laughed so much. I wish I could
remember what she called my mother.

Sheepcote Street was not a quiet neighbourhood, there were always
loud quarrels within and between families. On the whole though,
these disturbances stayed within understood limits. Even the
violence stopped at fists and sticks and was fairly predictable;
the neighbours did not knife each other. On one occasion we did
have two street gangs meet for a battle with bottles, bricks and
knives. This sort of thing was out of the ordinary and when it
happened we kept indoors.

Sarah Fare

Sarah deserves a chapter to herself because she was my Mother's friend for a good many years and left a deep impression on us. She was an enigma to Tommy and me but we looked forward to her visits and the 'magic' she amazed us with. She would have been in her 30s then, around Mother's age.

Sarah was a thin person who today would be described as slim and admired for it. At that time anyone who 'hadn't a lot of meat on 'em' was pitied because they had not had enough to eat. There were more thin people around than fat ones between the 1914 and 1939 wars. I think Sarah was naturally thin because she had very small features and slim legs and feet. A strange thing about her was that when she was sitting down her right foot would wag rapidly up and down. I was riveted by that wagging foot which went at a tremendous pace, and I tried to make my foot do the same.

Sarah had been married and probably still was when we knew her. She and Bill Fare had had a son who died in infancy; if he had lived things might have worked out differently. In those days couples did not, could not, divorce. When they parted, they just went their separate ways. Like Sarah and Bill, they might live in the same district and often pass each other without so much as a look, as if they were complete strangers.

Bill's family lived in Granville Street which was just around the corner from Sheepcote Street, and so far as I know, this is where Bill lived after he and Sarah parted. I saw him many times in and around Broad Street. He was a slight man and rather bent with a ready smile who was always very pleasant to me. I saw him at the library once and noticed that he was having difficulty getting down steps. When I told my mother she said, 'He's got rheumatics from the War'.

Bill was a hero in Mother's eyes, and with other returning soldiers had been given a hero's welcome by the Lord Mayor at the Town Hall. He had been a prisoner of war but escaped by hiding in a barrel and had suffered great hardship until he got back to his regiment. He may have been wounded because for a time he was in a hospital for wounded soldiers where Sarah took me a couple of times to visit him. Bill lay in a room with no more than three other beds, and while he and Sarah were talking I met some other visiting children. We investigated a radiator, something we had never seen before, discovered it had moving parts and spent some time unscrewing nuts.

Sarah was a quietly spoken person who seemed of higher intellect than my mother. She would talk to me about crossword puzzles; on one occasion she only missed finishing it by one word, she told me. I must have looked blank because I didn't know what she was talking about. If only she had shown me or told me about crosswords it might have helped me with my schooling.

Unlike my mother, Sarah did not think reading was a waste of time, and I think she was trying to encourage me to read because she once gave me a book. It was wonderful to have my own book, one I did not have to hurry over and return to the library before the expiry date. I burned some halfpenny candles reading *My Neighbour Raymond* in bed.

My reading up to this time had been solely what was acceptable to St Barnabas's Academy, and somehow I knew that a sixpenny novel from 'Woolies' would have been frowned upon, regardless of its content. Having said that, I read the book without understanding the story, just reading 'words'. I had a book and that was satisfaction enough; it was my only possession and I kept it for years. It probably ended its days on the fire since my mother would not have known any other use for it.

Sarah was a very neat person with an air of elegance. She was somehow different from anyone else we knew, and kind too. Tommy and I loved her. Her clothes were tidy and her blond hair was wound into her neck to make a bun. She wore a gold chain with a locket which consisted of a little picture frame with two pieces of glass held together with a gold band. The photograph it held was of Tommy, not me.

Everybody loved Tommy. After he died Sarah's visits became less frequent. I suppose that little picture she wore became a sad reminder of the little boy she had lost.

I never heard how Sarah earned her living. Some of my mother's friends worked in factories at polishing and other dirty jobs, but Sarah did not seem to work anywhere. I once heard my mother tell one of our neighbours, during a discussion about Sarah, 'She's too bloody idle to work, the lazy mare.'

43

There was one occasion when Sarah slept in lavatories at the back of houses in Oozells Street. She would not have been disturbed because few people braved going to the 'petty', as Gran called them, in the middle of a winter's night. In front of those 'lavs' was a brick wall then a 30 foot drop into a timber yard, leaving them exposed to the wind off the canal. Sleeping rough is not a new phrase

The next night Sarah came to our house telling my mother where she had slept and asking if she could stay with us. I remember how rough she had looked, unwashed, with her clothes crumpled. We had no bed in the attic, so Florrie shared the big bed with my mother and I slept in a small bed in the same room with Sarah.

This was the only time I can remember her sleeping in our house, and I remember because we lay in the dark eating chocolates. Sarah only gave me one, but I could hear the crackling of paper as she took them from a bag. She had kept the chocolates hidden from my mother, why else wait until we were in bed in the dark? I was content with the one chocolate and slept sweeter until morning, but I never told my mother about them. She would have told the neighbours and the subject would have been gossiped over again and again. I did not want Sarah to be in our Mom's bad books.

With no home and no job, where had Sarah got the money to spend on chocolates? I don't know, but she had probably sold a few boxes of matches before coming to sleep at our house. It seems she would stand by St Philip's Cathedral and ask passing gentlemen if they needed any matches. She must have struck lucky that night and sold quite a lot of boxes at a penny a box.

Suddenly, there was a man in Sarah's life and her fortunes seemed to change dramatically for the better. His name was Teddy Talbot and they lived together in a bed sitting room, which was not un-usual because lots of people had to share a house. Her address was now King Alfred's Place which was down Broad Street near the Hall of Memory. The house was owned by an elderly man, a Mr Pearce, who took in performers from the local theatres, so I suppose it was a boarding house.

To reach Sarah's room you went through the front door then crossed a room to a door which led into a small yard. You crossed the yard and entered another room to reach stairs which lead up to Sarah's room. I did not much like all this, especially the stuffed dog which I had to pass, but once up there we were in a different world. Sarah did not have to scrub her table, or varnish its legs with Shelac, (bought for three half-pence [1 1/2d = .625p] in a jam jar from Williams the Paint and Drysalters in Broad Street). She had come up in the world and the furniture in that room was lovely. There were big, well padded armchairs that you could have slept in and other things I was not to see again until I went to work at Upwood. Sarah usually had a bright fire burning in the grate, its flickering flames showing up the furniture and the big bed. That room seemed full of quality and luxury which left a deep impression on me, and somehow Sarah fitted in. This was her real station in life. I would have been happy living in those surroundings.

We have all striven for something in our lives, be it part of a hobby, a holiday or a posh car. Some people just want money to hoard for a rainy day, which for a hoarder never comes. All Sarah wanted was a place she could call home and someone to share it with.

I think Ted was a little older than Sarah. He was quiet and stocky with greying hair and had only one eye. I loved visiting them and listening to the records Sarah put on the gramophone. It was not the type with the big horn though it still needed to be wound up. She had some of the songs like, 'Stay Out Of The South', and 'She Do' Wanna, She Do' Wanna.' I have heard the first sung many times over the years -'If you don't like brown eyed beaut-iful girls, stay out of the south.' to a lively tune. I have never heard the other one since it was played at Sarah's.

You can understand my affection for Sarah. I was nor a demanding child, but she gave me what I was missing at my own home, under-standing and possibly love. She must have liked me being around and certainly understood me and my needs, which she showed by giving me her time. Sarah was not unpredictable and did not fly into rages. These visits were mainly without my mother, making them all the more enjoyable.

Why she and Ted left King Alfred Place, I don't know. It had seemed she was set up for life with everything anyone could wish for, and she did not have to work for it. My mother and I paid Sarah and Ted a visit at their new home in King Edward's Road near Camden Street. You can't imagine the contrast between that lovely room at the boarding house and this terraced house in a row of one down and two ups. Children ran around, neighbours stood on their steps and eyed us as we walked to Sarah's door. We were strangers, so we had to be watched and measured up.

Sarah was sharing a lavatory with her neighbours and would be allocated her day for washing in the brew house. You had to fit into the system if you wanted to live in peace.

This part of Ladywood had the reputation of being a rough quarter in a very poor district. These people knew what poverty meant and lived harsh lives trapped in depressing surroundings. Most were born into it and would die in it, just trying to make the most of their lives in between.

The house had an uneasy atmosphere and we could see that Sarah was not happy. She was grumbling at Ted for dropping crumbs on the floor, so we had obviously walked into a row. Ted sat at the table and never said a word, he just looked at the floor. Even when she called him a 'Bloody pig', he never stirred or retaliated. I had never seen this side of Sarah before. She had always been so calm and I would not have dreamed she had a bad temper.

I never saw Sarah again, but we did hear about her because bad news travels fast. Ted had been caught making counterfeit two shilling pieces [10p] and was sent to prison. We never learnt whether Sarah stayed at King Edward's Road or moved on.

The 'magic' Sarah used to perform for Tommy and me was very mysterious. She could take out her teeth and put them back again. Try as we might, we could not move our teeth, no matter how hard we pulled.

Other Friends

A man friend of my Mother's (she had lots of friends), worked at the brewery by the Crown. Bob Gibbs was thick set with broad shoulders, white, wavy hair, and a fresh complexion. I suppose you could have called him good looking. I disliked him intensely to the point of avoiding him at every opportunity. My mother had to be lead everywhere with me as her guide, and if I saw Bob in the distance I would turn around and go another way. But our mother was not stupid and she would ask, 'Who have you seen?' and I would reply, 'Nobody - it's better this way.'

I remember one night there was a group of people at our house. They were having a sing song and I dare say the ale was flowing. Bob was there and the woman he lived with who everyone called 'Polly McGra'.

That night she wore a cartwheel hat which was very much out of fashion. Bob hated the hat and offered me a shilling to dance on it [5p]. Imagine, a shilling, the price of a Sunday dinner, and I didn't need a bribe to dance. The hat was taken from Polly's head and put on the floor, then with much laughter from the audience I soon ruined it. What a rotten thing to do, poor Polly must have felt so humiliated, but I was only 8 or 9 years old. I don't remember being given the shilling.

Bob made quite a few visits without Polly. I awoke one night to hear voices. In the dark I heard my Mother asking a question and Polly's name was mentioned, and that hated man was where my poor, lovely Father should have been. He was gone before I got up for school next morning. After we moved to Sherborne Street, his night time visits stopped, even though Polly had died. Whether he called during the day I don't know.

Bob and Polly lived in Sherborne Street near Grosvenor Street West. Theirs was a little house up an entry behind the street and stood at the end of a row. A vast brick wall separated them from the flour mill. I know because I climbed it to see what was on the other side.

Polly died young and it was from this house that she was buried. The coffin lid was stood propped against the wall for a time and I noticed that the brass plate gave her name as 'Polly McGrath'. My mother and I went to see her before the funeral to pay our last respects. Poor Polly was only 28 years old. She was Irish with a round, rosy face and lovely dark curly hair. She came to England looking for a better life and ended her days working in the flock factory in Browning Street.

Flock was made from rags, old clothes, towels and discarded bedding which was torn and pulverised to make a cheap filling for beds, pillows and cushions. The air in the works was grey with dust from the tearing cloth, and Polly worked in those conditions for eight hours each day, five days a week and four hours on Saturday morning. No wonder she died when the stuff penetrated her lungs. When the factory was burned down the glow was better than any bonfire we had ever seen. As I watched from our bedroom window I thought of Polly and was glad to see it burning.

The last time I saw Bob Gibbs he was standing with his back against the bow (fire guard). As I walked into the house and saw him, I froze. He must have known how much I disliked him because he looked at me in an uneasy, uncomfortable way. I don't know how long he had been there but he just turned to my mother and asked, 'Can I stop the night?' She told him he couldn't, then added, 'Tek no notice of 'er', 'Er' being me. She went on to explain why he couldn't sleep with her at that particular time. He left abruptly, slamming the door, and I never saw him again. A few minutes later Mother told me that Bob had asked her to marry him. I wasted no time in letting her know that if she did, I would leave home.

My mother had lots of friends, men and women. If you went out you could be sure of bumping into somebody she knew, especially round the market area. There was one friend that I did like, an 'uncle' called George Spencer, known as Spunner.

Children very quickly form an opinion of people and either like them right away or dislike them intensely. I took to Spunner and I am sure that if he had married my mother life would have been easier for Florrie and me, though I can't say what his life would have been like with our Mom and her flaming temper. He was a reserved man who seemed younger than Mom, but I knew no more about him except that he lodged with a family in St Vincent Street.

We usually made a call on Spunner when the purse was empty, and he always saved the day with a hand out. It was me who had to do the rounds of the local pubs until I found him. I did not like a lot of the things that I had to do, but dare not complain. That would have brought a punch and a mouthfull of abuse, and I would still have to do what Mon wanted done.

Those trips were planned as carefully as if I were going on safari in the African jungle. I knew about Africa from library books. Hunters stalked their quarry until they made a kill, then brought home its stuffed remains as a rug, complete with head. Mom's strategy was to call me in from play, shut the door and pull or push me to the fireplace. She would sit on the old squab, look into my face and quietly give me my instructions. Yes, quietly, because she didn't want the neighbours to know what was going on. I don't know which was worse, our Mom in a flaming temper or quiet and menacing. Either way, I was liable to 'piddle me drawers' with fright.

The plan went this way. I was to go into the yard and after a while shout, so the neighbours could hear, that I was going to play on the Rec, or perhaps with one of my school friends in Essington Street? This would obviously put me out of earshot of Mom and served as my cover when I came back late, because I could not hear her calling.

First I would go to a pub at the corner of Ledsam Street and St Vincent Street, Spunner's usual haunt. I would push open the door and look round at the people seated there. If he was not in the first room I would try the next one. If I had no luck at that pub I would go down Ledsam Street to the Mitre. If he was not to be found in there either I would make my way back home, looking in at a couple more pubs on the way.

If Lady Luck was with me and I found him, Spunner would spring from his seat as soon as he saw me. He would come outside and I would ask, 'Could you let me mother have a couple of shillings?' No talk of borrowing a couple of bob until Friday when she will pay you back. Mom could not borrow because there was no way of paying back. I would go home absolutely elated because I had made a kill. Can you imagine a 2 shilling piece, 10 pence in today's money, making such a difference to your life? You had a dinner for the next couple of days.

Having found Spunner I would make my way home along the dark streets. I did not need to worry that I would get a hiding because Mom knew where I was. As I neared our yard I would hear my name being shouted, Mom had a good pair of lungs at this time in her life. I would shout back, 'I'm coming.' In the still quiet of the night our voices would echo and be heard streets away. This was part of the plan. The neighbours were meant to believe that 'Smith's girl' was playing her mother up by stopping out playing when all the other children were safely indoors. I would stop at the entrance to the yard and give one mighty blast, 'I'm coming.', pretend I had been running and gasp, '-I'm here, Mom', gabling a fictitious tale about where I had been and with whom and I how I had not known the time. You can be sure the neighbours heard all this, looked at their clocks on the mantelpiece and tut-tutted about the time.

The first thing she asked was, 'Had I found him?', then, 'How much did he give you?'. I would put the money on the table and go to bed.

Not all these excursions were fruitful. On one occasion when I was sent to find Spunner Mom wanted to come and I knew something was amiss. She had an aura about her and I was prepared for an explosion at any minute. These times were awful, I go tense writing about them, but I took her arm and off we went.

We went straight to the little pub on the corner of St Vincent Street and Ledsam Street to find Spunner in the first room. He followed me out and went up to my mother who was standing on the edge of the pavement. They started talking, or rather Mom was talking, George just stood listening. After a while he put his hand in his pocket, and brought out something which he offered her. She exploded, shouting that it was not enough and what could she do with it? She lashed out at him and the coins went up in the air and fell then onto the road. I bent down to gather them up but was pulled away and told, 'Tec me 'ome', leaving poor Spunner standing like a man in a dream.

Not long after this incident poor George met a sad end. He worked in the building trade and to get to his job in Harborne he had to go by bus. The story goes that he stepped off a bus into the path of a car. My mother bought a wreath for his funeral and we stood on the pavement among his neighbours and friends as the coffin was brought down the yard to the hearse. How sad I felt, I had liked Spunner.

Odd corners from the past. The canal company's stables in Sheepcote Street and the flour mill in Grosvenor Street West.

The Treacle Stick

Looking back on my childhood, they were such harsh times of poverty, sickness and loneliness, and there seemed no escape. It was a miracle that we survived, and we did so only because, in our desperation, we applied for Parish Relief. We knew it better as the 'Treacle Stick'.

The Board of Guardians of the Poor were part of the lofty and inaccessible system by which 'they' ruled our lives, moralising, capricious and cruel. When you applied to 'go on the Parish' it was because you had no means of any kind. You attended a hearing to be questioned by a bench of three comfortable, worthy, middle class people who were so far removed from your world that they might have come from China. You knew their power, they could feed or starve you. If there was any appeal from their judgement we never heard of it and would not have known how to use it.

After all your circumstances had been examined, and if you were accepted as a worthy claimant, you were allocated a weekly sum of money. This was to be taken in gratitude and humility, with many scrapings of feet on the doormat before and after the inquisition. It was to be to spent wisely, not squandered on luxury items, like a constant fire in the grate, clothes, shoes on your feet all year round and a good hot dinner every day.

To make sure you observed all the rules and were not making or getting money from another source, you were summoned before the Board of Guardians from time to time and interrogated. Questions were asked in clear, precise tones by stern, well fed faces which made notes of your answers and then judged you. I was on a knife's edge at any time with my mother, so you can imagine what it was like for me having her confronted by these awesome people. I was frightened that she might suddenly lose her temper and tell them, as she told many people, 'To stick it up your arse.'

You must have seen the picture of the little boy standing before a group of Roundhead inquisitors during our Civil War and being asked, 'When did you last see your Father?' I knew exactly how the child felt, almost speechless with fear like me confronted by the Guardians. Mother would vent her feelings about our benefactors as we walked home up Islington Row.

That summons from the Board was not all that happened when you were on the treacle stick, you also had someone to keep an eye on you. They were called many names, in fact everything in the farmyard apart from duck. They had almost complete power over the running of your lives with authority to enter your home at any time during 'office hours'.

We had a lady visitor who wore pince-nez; she was short and dumpy and very domineering, I will go further and say she was arrogant. Miss Parr once paid us a visit when I was at home. That was not unusual, I lost a lot of time from school because of poor health. In walked the 'Parish woman' to look us over. After a few questions she said she wanted to see the beds, and walked towards the door leading to the upper rooms. The first thing she saw was the pow on the stairs, unemptied. She turned on my mother, 'The urine should have been disposed of before now.'

As she went into the bedroom she could see Mom had not been lying when she said she had not had time to make the beds and empty the slops. Miss Parr turned over the bed clothes, pulling them out from the bottom of Mother's bed and mine to see that they were clean. No complaints on that score, my mother was certainly clean. As she left Miss Parr remarked fatuously, 'Don't forget to empty the chamber pot, Mrs. Smith.' Little did that lady know that under different circumstances our Mom would have emptied it over her.

On another occasion my sister Florrie came running up the yard and into the house to tell our Mom that Miss Parr had stopped her in the street and had lifted up her clothes to look at her 'knackers'.

It was no use objecting to Miss Parr, it was no use complaining, who would you complain to? In reality no one person was to blame, it was just Them, and us poor souls were Us. Miss Parr humiliated Florrie and my mother, and she was entitled to. Miss Parr had the power to stop our little bit of money. We were on her list and she had to see that our home and persons were kept clean at all times.

What an existence. We lived a day to day struggle for food and the other essentials of life. An empty grate was a depressing sight and I saw many of those, so we were cold. In winter we froze. We did not always have light. If we had no lamp oil then we used a candle standing on a saucer. They did not last long so they guided us up the stairs early. When we were in bed the candle was 'dowted' [dowsed] so that a stub was left to light us downstairs in the morning.

Clothes came from second hand clothes shops or neighbours. A good second hand clothes shop where you could mooch about until you found something suitable was like an Aladdin's Cave.

Another way of buying clothes and household linen was by 'checks'. When you opened a check account you agreed to pay a regular weekly amount to a collector and were given vouchers to a certain number of times its value, say ten times. This form of credit existed alongside pawnbrokers, moneylenders and what small shops would allow, and it still does. You could take your check to a shop or warehouse which accepted them and choose what you wanted. It was not cheap credit, but Florrie and I were kitted out by this method every Christmas. You should have seen us around about October, a couple of ragged urchins.

A roof over your head and your own place to come and go as you pleased was all important, so the rent always came first. The place was yours so long as you were a good payer, so 4 shillings and 8 pence and the rent book always lay on the table the day the agent called to collect.

There was no NHS in the 1920s and 30s so you had to pay for a visit to the doctor. However, if you were on the Parish you could see a doctor appointed by the Guardians free, and his consulting rooms were in Margaret Street in the centre of Birmingham. His name happened to be the same as ours, Smith, but he was just plain Smith whereas we were Barrett-Smith. Names made no difference to your status.

You waited your turn with parish and private patients to see this doctor. Only your address gave you away. Living in Sheepcote Street we had no status. Doctor Smith was a very bluff mannered man who was always in a hurry to get you out of his surgery, but perhaps in the circumstances he was doing his best. Many of the people in his care were suffering from malnutrition and lived in an environment which destroyed good health. If Doctor Smith could have dispensed fresh vegetables, eggs and fish, his work load would been cut to a fraction. Consumption (TB as it was later known) was rife, and with overcrowded housing, perhaps ten people living in a couple of rooms, infections rampaged.

If one child had measles the others would soon catch it, then it spread to next door and all round the yard.

Schools were overcrowded too, with as many as 48 in a class. I remember Florrie catching impetigo, a horrible complaint which produced sores all over her face. You had to be isolated because it was contagious. Dr Smith came to the house on that occasion and prescribed the appropriate jallop which in due course had the desired effect. Dennis Thacker caught it at one time and I suppose his mother had neglected to call the doctor earlier. When Dr Smith saw the state Dennis was in he said that if the child had been left much longer 'His ears would have fallen off.'

Once I ran out into the horse road just as a lad on his bike was passing our yard, and my feet got tangled up with the spokes of a wheel. I suffered the pain for a couple of days so my mother thought I had better see the doctor. I limped all the way up Sherborne Street and Sheepcote Street, down Broad Street and along Edmund Street to Margaret Street.

After hearing how I had hurt my feet, Doctor Smith gave his verdict. 'When I was a lad, I sprained my foot every week.' No advice was given and nothing prescribed, so I just hopped home and was in more pain when I got there than before I set out. A kindly word would have gone a long way, or even a suggestion that I rest my foot for a day or two. Having no official proof of my injury in the form of a doctor's note to cover my absence from school, I just had to get there.

The day before my mother died in 1934, Doctor Smith came to see her. He did not stay long but just looked at her, asking as left the bedroom, 'Is there anything you want?'. He was on the landing about to go downstairs when my mother asked, 'Have you got any dirty old pound notes?' That was our Mom, game to the last. Doctor Smith smiled as he left the house.

Hard Times

Mother's visits to the Eye Hospital and the Ear, Nose & Throat Hospital eventually ended after she had endured two unsuccessful operations on her eyes.

Before her condition reached this stage we tried everything we could. I was researching a 1924 *Evening Mail* at the Central Library when I saw an advertisement for an ophthamologist, or eye doctor as we called him. It was this same advert at a later date which led Mom to visit him at Chequers Walk. The incident stuck in my mind because he was Indian, there were few Indians in Birmingham then, and we could not pronounce his name. He told Mom he could cure her complaint but it would take some time. At 2 shillings [10p] or 2/6d a visit, this was impossible, but Mom would brood about it. It was almost certain she had the eye disease Glaucoma which was passed on to Florrie and myself, in which case the doctor may have been giving her false hopes.

On the advice of the consultant at the Ear, Nose & Throat Hospital, Mother was to have all her teeth extracted before she had any more treatment, and they all came out at one session.

I remember leading her home along the badly lit streets, walking from the light of one lamp to the next. Every so often she would take away the cloth she held and spit the blood from her bleeding gums into the gutter. It is a long walk from Bath Row up Bishopsgate Street and back to Sheepcote Street, and I still feel it was rather a terrible experience for a child. How my mother made it home I don't know, she must have felt very ill.

Mother did get home and lived to tell the tale, kept going by her indomitable spirit. She needed all of it for the next and last operation. Large red lumps had developed on each side of the bridge of her nose and she was told that she must have an operation. She would not have been given a reason or explanation.

When the letter arrived telling Mother the date of her operation it presented awful problems that no one today would even think of. We had hardly any clothes except the ones we wore day after day, and no nightwear. Going into hospital meant you needed night gowns, so to get them something had to be sold. But what?

We had only a few sticks of furniture of little or no value, so what could my mother do? The only thing left of any value at all was her mangle. She was proud of that machine and I dare say it had taken many, many weeks before it was finally paid for. I remember the name of the makers, Cox, stamped on the frame above the rollers. It went, and Mom bought two night gowns. The irony was she need not have sold the wringer because the hospital would have lent her a nightgown.

That operation removed the bridge of Mom's nose leaving a flat surface between her eyes, a terrible disfigurement. We can only guess why the operation was necessary because Mom would not have asked any questions of the medical staff. To ask a doctor what was wrong with you was unthinkable, so we remained in ignorance.

Before she went into hospital for this operation, as with all of them, Mother had to find someone to look after Florrie and me. On one occasion we had stayed with a neighbour, Mrs Newbold who had been friends with Mother when they were younger. I think it was providence that had brought them together again when she came to live in our yard. Lily Newbould was a good friend indeed, helping out when my father died and afterwards. While I was staying with them I went running, because I never walked anywhere, to the brew house where she was doing the weekly washing. Before she could warn me I kicked over the big copper kettle full of boiling water onto my left foot. For a good many weeks I limped to the Queen's Hospital for treatment, always by myself, and then onto school. I still have the scar.

During one of Mom's hospital stays I was not so lucky, I had to go into a 'home'. Every girl and boy dreaded this. The threat from your mother that she might put you there was enough to stop whatever you were doing. I found myself in Summerhill Homes for about two weeks, whilst Florrie was sent to the nursery at Lodge Road. During this time Florrie had an operation in the Children's Hospital, though we never fully understood what it was for.

Summerhill Homes was not a home where children stayed for years, but a short stay or a receiving home for children whose parents were temporarily unable to look after them. It was very strange. We had three uncles, an aunt and a grandmother in the area, the aunt and Gran living opposite our yard in Essington Street, but none of them offered to help.

56

My first day in the home was spent in isolation, which the other children said was because I might have had something catching. A lot of the time I sat by a window crying. The glass was frosted so I could not see outside and I felt shut out from the world.

When I woke up on the first morning of my stay two women had just entered the bedroom. I can't remember how many children shared it. I sat bolt upright in bed and cried, 'I've wet the bed'. That bed wetting went on for quite a few years, yet I don't think I had even done it before that night.

Summerhill Homes was like a cross between an isolation hospital and a prison. Our only contact with the outside world was on Sunday morning. For this we were dressed in clothes doled out from some obscure closet by a lady known as 'Mother May', without regard to quality or fit. Most of us were given woolly Tam O' Shanters and I had a lot of trouble with mine. It kept falling over my eyes so I could not see where I was walking and spent most of the time holding it on my head.

Our Sunday walk was not a long one. Walking in pairs and not talking, we travelled a dismal square of streets which I remember passed the Fire Station and Legge Street.

The thought of running away crossed my mind but I had no one to run to, so I soldiered on with the rest of the poor little souls. I was not going to live in a home indefinitely but the rest of them knew they would be sent on to long term institutions, such as Marston Green. I had better hopes because my Mom was only in hospital.

One evening a nasty trick was played on me. Some child came to tell me that my mother had come to take me home. I followed the bearer of the good news and found myself in the kitchen with the other children laughing at me, enjoying the nasty prank. I was told I had to help with the washing up, so I got on with it. The kitchen smelt of dirty soapy water. This is where I learnt about crickets. They were singing away up amongst the pipes that ran round the walls near to the ceiling.

Our education was not neglected and the hours spent in school were interesting. I remember reading to a lady who was sitting at a desk in what seemed a very large room. When you lived in a tiny terraced house, any other rooms seemed big. There was a fireplace with a fireguard in front of a lovely fire, and over the mantle was a picture of Jesus Christ surrounded by small

children. After morning lessons we had a dinner break followed
by a short afternoon session, then it was time for freedom and
play. I don't remember there being any toys to play with, though,
and I certainly never saw a book outside the schoolroom. I wanted
to be outside, going somewhere. Most of all I longed to go to the
library and to come home walking on air with my chosen book.

It was not a pleasant two weeks. I was safe, fed and kept clean,
with clothes to wear and shoes on my feet, but I was like a bird
in a cage. Being shut up day after day when I had been used to
my freedom had a profound effect. I wonder whether my fear of
being shut away, claustrophobia, began there?

'Come on, you're going home. Your mother has come for you.'
I was spellbound. The first words I spoke as I stepped tearfully
into the street were, 'I'll never cheek you again, Mom.' As we
walked out of Summerhill Terrace we came to a little shop where
Mom bought me some sweets. There was no kiss or hug of welcome and no conversation as we walked home. But my prayers
that night were longer than usual. Added to 'Please God, let
me get up early for school in the morning' was, 'And don't
let me wet the bed. Amen'

Daily Mails

One of the worst things about poverty like ours that we went
short of footwear. Florrie and I had new shoes at Christmas,
but during the summer we had to wear Dunlop pumps because
our shoes would have worn out and we would have outgrown
them. Sometimes we were lucky enough to get a reasonable
pair of shoes from one of the many secondhand shops around
the district. Unfortunately I had very narrow feet and a shoe
that would seem comfortable to most children fitted me like
a barge.

For many others it was worse, they might have no shoes at all
during the wet and freezing winters. It was especially hard for
the big families. Shoes were something you could not hand down
from child to child because they wore out. Without money to get
them repaired at the cobblers many fathers repaired shoes themselves, and mothers too. I remember Mrs Newbold cobbling on
a last attached to a piece of timber, which might have been an
old table leg.

If luck was on your side you might get some help through a scheme run by the *Daily Mail* newspaper. I can't remember the details, but they contributed to a fund to provide footwear, stockings and clothes for the poorest children.

Anyone issued with a card for a pair of boots went to the distribution centre at the back of Digbeth Police Station. I remember a large lady glancing at my feet and sitting me down on a bench. She put a pair of boots into my hand, I put them on and stood up. That was it, I was kitted out. The large lady also gave me a pair of long, thick, itchy black stockings. At first girls were issued with the same as boots boys, but later were given shoes.

Those boots were hard, black leather lace ups, amazingly heavy and built to last. They would have suited Klondyke gold miners standing in icy rivers panning for gold. Each boot was marked near the cuff with a circle of small, perforated holes to prevent them from being pawned. I must have looked just like Minnie Mouse in mine, with skinny little legs in black tubes. I could not just put those boots on and walk, I had to practice lifting one foot at a time.

On our way home with our boots we passed Williams's, the paint and colour merchants. It said so in painted letters over the windows of their Broad Street shop. Here we bought a penny tallow candle which was softened by the fire and rubbed over the boots to make them more pliable and comfortable to wear.

Socially, you were marked by your 'Daily Mails', and the better off children would look at you as though you had two heads. 'Why is she wearing those?' Worse, our school was of the old type with separate classrooms and playgrounds for boys and girls. There would have been more than one pair of Daily Mails running around the boys' playground and kicking tin cans after school, but I was usually the only wearer in the girls' area. Daily Mail's looked alright on a boy, they were made for them, strong and tough.

They were good boots but they had disadvantages. You could not stand on your toes, or dance, or twirl your partner around in the English country dance session. It would have looked and sounded like a cart horse in clogs. People could hear you coming in your Daily Mails, they made such a clonking sound on the floor boards. I had dry feet, its true, but I also endured blisters on my toes and heels caused by the boots being too big or too small.

*Summerhill Homes,
now a day centre for
the elderly.*

*Nellie and Florrie
in 1928. Florrie
is holding her
special handbag,
see page 62.*

The *Daily Mail* distributed more than boots, there were also clothes. But they were only given to destitute children and I never had them, proving that I was not poor enough. Girls got high necked, long sleeved, navy blue jumpers which were called 'ganzys' and a thick, navy blue skirt. The name ganzy came from the heavy, oiled wool sweater worn by Guernsey fisherman. Boys had similar pullovers and short trousers coming just to the knee.

So were the poor set up for winter, through the caring people who contributed to the Daily Mail Fund. Being grateful did not stop me from hating them.

Chilblains were one result of unsuitable footwear. They were a scourge and cost many days of schooling. Children's feet were mainly affected but adults could get chilblains on their hands, making their fingers red and swollen. Chilblain's itched and almost drove you mad. The skin on my heels and toes has been broken through scratching, but the more you scratched, the worse it got. At these times when you had no option but to wear your boots and make your way painfully to school.

There did not seem to be a cure for chilblains, but there was something which did ease them, and that was urine. I have sat with my feet in a chamber pot in my own urine and found relief from the burning itching in my feet, and I'll bet I was not the only one who took 'the waters' cure.

Christmas at Home

One year I joined the Christmas Club run by Odam's, the local general store, and put into it the pennies [.4p] and half-pennies I was given by the neighbours for running errands. I was going to buy our Christmas Day tea. It must have taken months for me to save enough money, but when the time came there was between 1 shilling and 6 pence [7.5p] and 2 shillings [10p]. I splashed out on a tin of pineapple chunks, some real cream, which I didn't like at all, and some butter, which was a luxury. Usually we had margarine, or 'maggy-ann', on our bread, and if we had jam then the maggy-ann was left off. I think I had some tea, because you could get small quantities at these shops in areas where people could not afford to buy half pounds. All this was used for one meal between the three of us, Mother, Florrie and me.

I also bought a special present to put in Florrie's Christmas stocking, a pillow case which was never more than half full. Playing Father Christmas to her was was play acting which I enjoyed, sharing a closely guarded secret known only to Father Christmas himself, or in our house, herself. Florrie's present that year of 1928 was a handbag full of sweets. What a treat she had. If you look closely at the pictures on page 60 you can just make out the edge of that bag in Florrie's right hand. Pouch shaped and hung from a cord, it was not made from some rich material such as velvet or silk and it did not shine or glitter, it was made of tin. But to Florrie it was wonderful and she loved it, a Christmas present to remember. I bought a similar bag for my school friend Lizzie Henley, who died aged about 14.

Christmas Day would be bleak for some children and no different from any other day. For them there was no waking up at dawn to empty the pillowslip and shouting, 'He's been, Mom, and look what he's brought me.' The usual presents consisted of a blood orange, a russet apple, a new penny and a few mixed nuts. Why a blood orange and a russet apple, I don't know, but they were expected, in season and very welcome.

People had such a great sense of humour, it kept them from brooding about the hardships they were enduring. So in a family someone always had a 'joke' Christmas stocking. If there was a dad he would get it. It was a message not of goodwill, but of hope, that of Mom hoping for a cup of tea in bed. From his stocking dad would pull a crumpled page of the Mail, Despatch or the Buff, a few sticks of firewood, some coal and a box of matches. He got the message and went down to light the fire and put the kettle on. Dad's stocking was good for a laugh long after Christmas.

One Christmas when I was about 9 years old we had a windfall. A small postcard told my mother that she had been allocated a Christmas Dinner. I just can't tell you the relief and joy that card brought, it meant the difference between a feast or more breast of lamb. Only the very poor were ever given these tickets. There were plenty of those but many were eliminated when other family circumstances were taken into account.

On Christmas Eve we were up at the crack of dawn to join the hundreds of others fetching their dinners. I was despatched clutching that precious little card with instructions and threats of, 'Don't bleeding well give it to anybody or lose it.' As if I would give it away, and how could I lose it? I clenched the card so tightly that my fingers would have had to be wrenched open. We were still in Sheepcote Street and the distribution centre was at the Drill Hall in Thorpe Street down the Horse Fair, which was quite a distance.

When I saw the crowds in Thorpe Street I couldn't believe it. People were on the move down the Bull Ring, some going down, others with their loaded bags elbowing their way up, but all I saw was a mass of bodies milling around the doors. I don't know how long I stood or how I got to the front, but suddenly a very big man in uniform appeared and started giving orders, 'All ticket holders queue here and the rest, move back.' When he was satisfied, the big gates swung open and we moved in single file into a cavernous brick building.

Inside were rows of trestle tables piled with Christmas food. The first thing we were given was a big brown paper carrier bag which we held open for the helpers to drop in whatever was on their table. I remember a loaf of bread, a piece of beef, tea and sugar, and a small block of something like chocolate. There was a lot more and my bag was full and heavy. I can't remember which route I took to get home, but I stopped at the bottom of Sheepcote Street to have a rest. My hand mooched in amongst the things in the bag and, yes, at the bottom was a packet of chocolate. Talk about 'Corn in Egypt', it was too much of a temptation.

As I got nearer to our yard I started to be afraid of what Mom would say and do about the missing chocolate. As I staggered into the house I blurted out, 'There was some chocolate as well, but I was hungry so I ate it.' She was taking things from the bag and putting them on the table but never looked up, just saying 'That's alright'.

That Christmas was one of our good ones. We had enough food in the cupboard not to worry about our next meal. But there had been people as needy as ourselves waiting outside the Drill Hall without tickets, hoping for some surplus food. As I left the hall with my heavy bag I had seen our next door neighbour, Mrs Thacker. She was leaning on her crutches and had probably been standing for hours. I know she did not get anything because we saw her come home empty handed.

Playtime

Life had its bright spots which helped me to forget what happened at home. I loved babies, and in our yard was a lovely boy called Tony. His mother, Ruth, used to let me take him out in his big, posh pram which I loved pushing. It made me feel quite grown up. I was still only 12 or 13 at the time but I must have been capable for a mother to entrust her baby to me. I would not allow anybody near Tony, and if one of the kids asked if they could have a push of that magnificent pram the answer was a definite no, though they could join me for a walk with it.

I usually walked along St Vincent Street, turned right into Ladywood Road then left at the New Park as it was known, being officially Chamberlain Park. After this I would go up Monument Road towards the Ivy Bush pub. There was a picture house on the other side of the road and our next door neighbours, the Spratts, could boast that their father had helped build it. My perambulation continued along Hagley Road to Five Ways, from where we had a choice of routes home.

Going for a walk was sometimes the only way to get out of the house. Our Mom never let me out alone at night except when I was on a special errand such as getting money from Spunner, but with the Bishop sisters and one or two other girls, she didn't mind. With 'Don't be late back' ringing in my ears, I would run down the yard to freedom.

We were noisy and boisterous. The girls were as rough as any boy and I could hold my own against the best of them. We played football in the street until the neighbours got fed up with the ball bouncing off their doors and threatened what they would do if we broke a window. This would quieten us down for a time while we played some less vigorous game.

The people living in the these streets had a great deal to put up with from the children, but they were the only place to play unless you lived near a recreation ground or a park. You could not play ball games in a park but had to 'Keep Off The Grass'. How pointless. Many had swings and roundabouts but they were mostly for younger children, and we had to make sure we were not caught by the 'parkie'.

We played jacks, or jackstones, which in different versions seems to have been played all over the country. First you collected five stones slightly bigger than marble size and sat in a ring with the jacks in the centre. Any number could play. The first player picked up the stones in their fist, then carefully opened it and threw them into the air. Since they would next have to pick them up again, this needed care. If you threw too hard the stones would go all over the place and you would never control them. The art came in as the stones fell, when you caught as many as you could on the back of your hand.

Now, you reversed the action, throwing the stones up and trying to catch them in your open hand. The idea was to catch all five stones, and if you did you could go on to the next stage.

You held four stones in your fist and one between your thumb and index finger. This one you threw into the air, then quickly put the four on the ground and caught the falling stone before it hit the ground.

In practice you would not usually catch more than two or three stones on the back of your hand. In this case you had to hold them whilst throwing one in the air, scooping up one or more stones from the ground, then catching the airborne stone before it fell. You went on until you had them all in your hand.

Jacks certainly tested your reflex actions. Some fell by the wayside in the early stages and so went off to find amusement elsewhere.

Another of our games was Tip Cat, for which you needed a bat and a 'cat'. You could not just go to a shop and buy a cat, it had to be made, and very proud was the lad who had whittled away for hours to produce one. The first requirement was a thick piece of wood about six inches long and a sharp knife. Slivers were laboriously whitled away to form a tapering cylinder an inch or more thick. This peg was thrown at the batter who had to strike it before it hit the ground. The winner was the one who hit the cat furthest, measured by counting the number of strides to it. Each of us would have several goes and the winner was whoever scored the most strides. You can bet there was skullduggery involving long or short strides, depending on who the strider wanted to win.

Like jacks, this game took quick reflexes and a sharp eye. Before the striker hit the cat we all backed away because if you were hit by a flying cat it would hurt. If the batter was a novice they could easily send it into the watching crowd, and nearby windows were frequent casualties. Of all the dangerous games we played, this was the worst.

None of our games involved money because we didn't have any, and except for balls, the equipment was home made. Even balls could be made up if someone had a pig's bladder, cost - 1 penny. You could have great fun with one of these, chasing other kids and hitting them over the head with it, especially if it was filled with water. Bladders would not stand up to rough handling and before long somebody got wet.

The simplest of our activities was bowling hoops. That is what they were, circles of iron which you slapped with your hand to send it bowling along as you ran to keep up. You got a very grimy hand. I have seen pictures of Victorian and Edwardian children bowling hoops, mostly little boys dressed in sailor suits with straw hats. The pictures showed a child running with a hoop but did not show an extra contrivance. This was a wooden handle with an iron loop at the end through which the hoop passed, which allowed you to guide and steer it. I have never seen a picture of a little girl with a hoop, perhaps bowling was thought too boisterous for girls.

If you possessed a 'bowl', as we called them, then a knock on your door, followed by 'Are you going to bring your bowl out?' was an invitation to a brisk half hour of physical and mental stimulation. The harder you pushed, the faster the thing would go, so you had to be careful not to frighten the horses on the road or the people on the pavement. Although many hoops were only rusted old bicycle wheels, somebody loved them. Even so, they would likely as not end up in the cut, the graveyard of bowls.

Bedsteads and Steam Lorries

The Orthopaedic Hospital stood on the corner of Sheepcote Street and Broad Street, and next to it was a cobbler's shop which made special boots for some of the patients. On the opposite corner of the junction stood the ornate and elegant stone entrance to a bank, I was so pleased on my last visit to Sheepcote Street in 1989 to find that it had not been pulled down.

Walking down Sheepcote Street on the same side as the bank you came first to the farrier's. I have seen lovely horses in the little yard waiting to be shod, not the heavy working horses which pulled carts around, but finer, quicker carriage horses. In the 1920s there were motor cars and lorries about but they were still few and expensive. Most goods travelled in a cart and all funeral hearses and coaches were pulled by horses. When they went we could no longer make a penny for a bucket of horse manure from someone with a bit of garden.

Next to the farrier's was Gilbert & Mellish. They worked in conjunction with the Hospital, and the shop window displayed irons of varying lengths to support legs which could not support their owners. We used to describe these unfortunate people as cripples, and the Orthodpaedic Hospital is still referred to by some older Birmingham people as the 'Cripples' Hospital', though it is now a pub.

A narrow yard or entry separated Gilbert & Mellish from Odam's, a name written in the concrete of the front step. I suppose you would call them grocers and chandlers because they sold every household thing you can think of: matches, washing powder, blue rinses, soap, bread, tins of fruit, cream to have with it, butter and so on.

If you do not know all about the washing of clothes in the 1920s and into the 1950s, blue rinses were the essential aid to making your washing look white. Modern washing powders contain things which have much the same effect. Then you bought 'Reckitt's Blue', a little round block wrapped in gauze which was dunked into the last rinsing water to give it a blue tinge. When the articles were hanging on the line you could tell who was the professional. The poor woman who had been too heavy on the bluebag could not wait for her next turn in the brew house to boil out the excess colour.

The Birmingham District Counties Bank offices were built in 1898 by local architects.

This quest for whiteness was courageous but doomed. Surrounded as we were by light and heavy industry, factory chimneys and railway engines belched black, sooty smoke, and the newly washed clothes would soon be peppered with black specs. We breathed this atmosphere with every breath. If you tried to remove one of the specks it spread itself and left a black smudge. Instead you waited until the clothes had dried then gave them a good shake, hoping that the bits of soot would fall away.

It seems strange that there were no coloured sheets or pillow slips, and that most towels, shirts, collars, separates and underwear were defiantly white. A baby was always dressed in white, from its vest, napkin, pilch, binder and underskirt to its long dress. I don't know if this was due to the cost of dyed cloth, or because the dyes in use were not colour fast, or just because of habits of social conformity which were so much stronger than people today can imagine.

Next down the street from Odam's came The Tap, a small public house with just a bar room. It was run by Mrs Brookes, a war widow who had a young boy and girl and was always referred to as the 'Missus'. One day The Tap closed down and the Brookes family moved on.

There was an entry separating the bar of The Tap from the tenant's dwelling quarters which led to a small building at the back which housed two modest businesses. Madame X made fancy cakes while Initial Towels laundered the roller towels used in offices and factories.

Between The Tap and our yard was a piece of waste land which was screened from the street by hoardings covered in advertising posters. They urged us to buy Monkey Brand to clean the brasses and Sunlight Soap to wash our hair, body and anything covering it. Lively Polly was a washing powder used in the copper, or boiler, and Campo was a blanco for whitening canvas pumps and soldiers' and sailors' webbing. The khaki variety used by the Army was given the timeless name of 'bullshit', though not by its makers. Of all these useful things, only Cherry Blossom Boot Polish is still sold. The billboards also advertised theatres and cinemas, and there were plenty of both in the 20s and 30s.

After the pub came Baylis's tube works, and we lived in its shadow, noise and smell. I can't say what their tubes were used for, so will skip quickly past.

After a couple of houses separated by an entry was a shop which, like Odam's, sold just about everything. It was to this shop that I was sent with the food voucher we once had from the Guardians. Nobody liked the proprietor, a surly individual who gave short weight when you bought sweets. In my case it did not happen often because such luxuries were rare, but the news got around so that many people did not go there.

Baker's, the paper shop, came next. When I was about 3 years old there was an incident involving Mrs Baker and myself. I have no memory of it, but it seems she was delivering newspapers in our yard and I was playing outside. For some reason she started to run towards me, I ran to the house, rushed through the open door, slipped and hit my face on a chair. It was very badly bruised. My father ran after Mrs Baker in a fury, and it was said she never came up our yard again.

One of the Baker sons was disabled and wore a built up boot on one foot, but he always appeared to be happy, always smiling. Perhaps business was good or he had decided to accept what the cards had dealt him and get on with living.

Going down Sheepcote Street on the same side as the Orthopaedic Hospital you passed the hospital cobbler's and came to Riley's, bedstead makers. Bedsteads then could be quite elaborate, especially the brass ones. In our house we had humble and heavy cast iron.

The big doors of Riley's warehouse opened onto our street and a horse and cart would be waiting to carry bedsteads to furniture shops all over the City. The floor was covered in straw and I remember the sweet smell when those doors were open. Children who happened to be around would gather on the pavement to see the goings on, often getting in the way, and being told to 'Op it'. It was a busy scene. The loading involved many comings and goings and the horse which pulled the cart had to be watched to make sure it didn't bolt. A runaway horse was a frightening sight and it took a brave man to stop one. To keep horses quiet a nose bag was hung over their necks with an opening just under the mouth, so they could feed.

Next to Riley's was Skinner's milk shop, then the house of Mr Hitchman, a retired police officer. Living next door were the Morris family whose boys were at the canal when Tommy fell into the water. Next came Giles's sweet shop. Mrs Giles had an owl which sat on a perch in the living room and looked at you with big round eyes. I loved to go into the shop just to see that bird.

Edgington's rag shop was next door, on the corner of Sheepcote Street and Essington Street. It seemed that nothing was ever sold from the premises, though there were piled mounds of old clothing with just enough room between to reach the living quarters behind. The half acre of the recreation ground, or Rec, lay between Ess - ington Street, Sheepcote Street and Grosvenor Street West.

Opposite the Grosvenor Street side of the Rec lived the Normans, my Uncle Ernie's family. It was not a shop though his mother sold a few sweets from an untempting array of boxes in the window. They were a side line because the Normans took in lodgers.

On the end of the Norman's house, bordering on Sheepcote Street, was a small workshop know to us as 'The Ferral' where they made metal tips for umbrellas and walking sticks. There was no demand in our area because I can't remember seeing anyone carry either article.

Some of the Normans were enterprising folk. A Mrs Norman living in Essington Street used to make and sell toffee apples. What profit she made during the week by standing over a cauldron of bubbling brown goo was all lost at the weekend. Every Saturday lunchtime her husband got drunk and threw coppers into the road for us kids to scramble after. He was very popular, unlike his brother Ernie.

At the other end of the Norman's property along Grosvenor Street was a blacksmith's. I loved to watch him hammering away with sparks flying everywhere, but ready to dodge if any came too near. The little shop was a blaze of light from the furnace and it must have been like working in an oven, even though the top half of the stable door was always open. The lower half was for leaning on when people stopped for a chat or just to look.

You can forget Wordsworth's glamourised blacksmith who worked under the spreading chestnut tree. This one was not a mighty man with large and sinewy hands, nor did his muscles stand out on mighty arms like iron bands. Our smith was small and rotund. He must have had muscles due to the nature of his work, but a little ditty of the day, 'The muscles of his brawny arms - Stood out like knots in cotton', fitted better.

Old factories in classical and gothic styles still stand on the south side of Sheepcote Street, tatty but interesting. The north side is dominated by a row of new and boring three storied, dutch gabled houses, probably made of plastic.

Sheepcote Street, with Foxall's Cafe centre and The Albion pub right. now demolished.

Quality wrought ironwork in Sheepcote Street is ignored and degraded.

Oozells Street North.

Photo: courtesy B'ham Housing Education Initiative

One day the forge doors remained closed - the blacksmith had died in a tram on his way home from work. I always felt sad about it and missed the forge, which never reopened.

Amidst all the dirt and grime and noise was the last thing you might expect to find, something suggesting green fields a long way from Grosvenor Street West; we had a flour mill. Fronted by an open space, it had large double doors to which lorries would go to be loaded with sacks of flour for delivery to local bakers.

These lorries were of a kind that you never see today, steam lorries. I thought until recently that they must have been tottering antiques even in the 1920s, but it seems not. My editor tells me that we must give a few details so as not to disappoint boys of all ages, so he has added the next bit to made me look like an expert of steam lorries.

There were eight British makers between the 1880s and the 1930s, but the two leaders were Foden and Sentinel. By the 1920s steam lorries were far from outdated, the best were efficient, economical, powerful and almost silent. The most up to date had gravity fed, self stoking firegrates. What finished them in the 1930s was not their performance, but crippling regulations and a heavy road tax. As late as 1950 Sentinel supplied 250 lorries to Argentina. From pictures I can say quite certainly that the lorries serving our local flour mill had the special cab shape of Sentinels.

Steam lorries were not fast, but life was lived at a slower pace. Their chug-chugging reached your ears before you saw the funnel with its curl of smoke and steam. If you were playing in the road you had ample time to get clear. Slung beneath and to the front of the vehicle was a tray to catch red hot cinders. It did not matter if they fell on a cobbled street, but many roads were surfaced with tar and chippings which the heat would have melted. I can remember the street bonfires on 5th November. What fires. They were being fed by the tar, of course.

There were more factories and offices in the lower part of Sheepcote Street of which I know little. One had a sign over a doorway which read 'M.M.M', whatever that meant. Our next door neighbour, Mr Eaton, worked in one of those factories but not on manual work. He came home looking as neat and clean as when he left. 'His' offices boasted a beautiful brass nameplate on the wall and a commissionaire at the door.

He stood resplendent in dark blue Corps of Commissionaires uniform, a leather belt across his chest from shoulder to waist to hold a purse and gleaming black boots. He was alert to open the door for callers, with one white gloved hand on the shiny handle and the fingers of the other hand touching the peak of his white crowned hat. The Corps was established in 1859 to help find work for ex-service men. This one was certainly a credit to his former regiment and an asset to his employers. To us he was not deferential but commanding. When he said 'Op It', we did, we knew our place.

In contrast to all this splendour, there was a coffee shop on the ground floor of this building which was popular with the local workers for cups of tea and bacon sandwiches.

Apart from shopkeepers there were few people who actually lived in this part of Sheepcote Street. The Laukes's lived next to the coffee shop. They had a teenage son called Tommy who suffered from what we called 'sleeping sickness'. He was always very well dressed, clean and tidy and often used to visit Mrs Allen in our yard to sit on a chair beside the fire. All cooking was done on the fire and Mrs Allen was a great believer in stews. Perhaps she couldn't cook anything else.

One day Tommy was sitting there when his illness caused him to doze off, leaning nearer and nearer to the fire and the stew pot. The contents needed constant stirring to prevent it from burning, and it was during a good stir that Tommy's foot was splashed by the boiling liquid. I don't think it was serious but it woke poor Tommy who ran from the house and never returned.

There was a girl at my school from in Grosvenor Street West who also had sleeping sickness. Her movements would get slower and slower until she slumped over the desk in a sort of coma. Eventually she stopped coming to school.

I have been told that it was probably Narcolepsy, an inherited condition which causes sleep episodes several times a day. It can now be controlled quite well with drugs deleveloped in the 1960s.

Also at this end of Sheepcote Street and facing Nile Street was the pub known locally as 'Goose's'; I never heard it called anything else. This was where my troublesome Uncle Tom drank when he was at home. It was at Goose's that he got his Dutch courage on the night he broke into our house and frightened us half to death.

Apart from one yard where few people lived, all the buildings
on this side of Sheepcote Street were offices and factories to
the end, where it met St Vincent Street. It was the same on the
opposite side up to Oozells Street North, on the corner of which
was an off licence.

The various businesses made their small local deliveries by
those delivery bikes with big square baskets fixed to the front,
or sometimes special containers for other goods. You could
gauge the scale of a business by the number of bikes it ran.
Madam X and this branch of Initial Towel for instance, had
only one apiece.

If at any time one of these vehicles was left unattended in the
street during a delivery or collection, the delivery lad might
expect to run half way down Sheepcote Street to fetch it back.
It was not unusual for one or more of the local kids to fancy a
ride. They would peddle off like fiends with the delivery lad
shouting after them at the top of his voice and boxes of Madame
X's best strew across the pavement. Once he had recovered his
bike the red faced, panting lad would have to work faster at
his round to catch up lost time.

It was not only the boys who took liberties. I once thought I
would like to have a go on the bike. Sad to say it was too heavy
and I couldn't get the pedals to turn. Worse, the owner saw me
and charged down the entry like a bull. I couldn't ride a bike -
but I could run.

Odam's was one of the shops that I had most to do with. It was
run by Mrs Odam and her daughter, Nellie. Mrs Odam was a
superior type of lady who would have fitted well in Upwood.
She always dressed in black with a broad, black velvet band
around her throat, she was quietly spoken and carried an air
of quiet authority.

That colour, black, was everywhere. Was it because there were
so many deaths? People did die younger and close relatives were
expected to wear mourning clothes for at least a year afterwards.
Widows certainly did. Another reason might have been that after
paying for a funeral you would have no money left, so it was a
case of wearing what clothes you had.

I was always running, especially when I was sent on an errand. The last words from Mom as I went through the door were always, 'And 'urry up, don't tek all bleeding day.' I would arrive at wherever I was going out of breath, then pour out my message in what could have been my last dying breath.

Monday was wash day in the brew house and the same items were always sent for, so I dashed into Odam's shop gasping, 'Can me Mom 'ave half a pound of Sunlight Soap, a packet of Rinso and a Blue,' and added, 'On the strap, please.' Nellie was serving.

Perhaps she had been on her feet for a long, busy time or perhaps her chilblains were playing her up. The poor girl's hands used to be so swollen and chapped that she usually wore woollen gloves with the fingers cut down. My sudden entry was not welcome. There I was, hanging on the edge of the counter gasping for air when I realised that I was not the only person in the shop. There were others waiting to be served, and ready to pay with real money.

The 'strap' meant that at the end of the week a little strip of paper would be handed to me showing what items my mother had purchased and the price. Under the total would be the message, 'Tell your mother this is what she owes.' I would convey Nellie's request to 'pay now', only to be told, 'Goo and tell 'er, 'arseole, I'll pay when I've got it,' meaning when she fetched her widow's pension from the post office.

The next time I went into Odam's Nellie said what she thought about me dashing in and expecting to be served in front of others, and above all, 'Asking for the strap.' Did she think that request lowered the tone of her establishment? I wonder if the waiting customers knew what I was talking about. Perhaps she felt slighted having to serve poor people.

Having to give credit must have been annoying for the shopkeepers, who liked to take a moralising approach to borrowing. But sales on the strap must have formed a large part of their sales which they would have lost if they refused to give it. They must have had a hard time making a living with so many little shops in competition. Their work involved standing in cold, draughty places for ten or more hours a day, occasionally nipping into the back room to warm their hands at the fire. And each sale would put only a few pennies into the till,

The Odams were really quite nice to us and Mrs Odam once gave Mother a hat, black of course. It was made from shiny material and had a large brim. I loved that hat and often tried it on. What I liked best was the bunch of bright red cherries stitched to one side. Hats were worn in those times, and it seems bizarre that in many circles it was thought rather shocking for an adult to go out without one.

Perfume was a luxury in the 1920s, as was scented soap. We used the same soap to wash anything and everything. But Mrs Odam used perfume and she gave me the empty bottles. They were pretty, glass stoppered bottles which retained their sweet smell. I loved those bottles and it did not matter at all that they were empty.

Nellie Odam lived at home with her mother. Like many thousands of other young women, her 'young man' had been killed in the war. Some did marry, but not Nellie. I remember her looking at a baby in its pram and saying that she would have had a child if only her fiance had come back.

They were such sad times. Girls cried over lost lovers, mothers mourned lost sons and widows struggled to raise orphans. Great Britain lost some six million men, but those who survived those four terrible years were, if not physically wounded, mentally scarred. Many ended up in mental hospitals, like Dick Field, a relative of my Grandmother's family who lived in Essington Street. He would be home for a while, then back in hospital again, but I can't say what the outcome was.

All the misery and the slaughter on both sides is hard to imagine. Germans too lived in trenches like rats and had girlfriends, wives, mothers and fathers.

Broad Street and the Walking Pigs

We were lucky living so near to Broad Street. If there was nothing to amuse us, such as settling a score with one of our 'friends' - 'I'll never play with you again,' or we got tired of the swings in the Rec, we could go up Broad Street and look in the shop windows. There were some good shops, too, and such a variety. On the corner of Oozells Street and Broad Street was a car salesroom. I remember seeing a car in that window with a notice stating that it had once belonged to King Edward VII.

The Crown (top)
still stands but
The Granville
has gone.

Photos: courtesy B'ham Housing
Education Initiative

Sentinel 6/8 ton four wheeled steam lorry of 1925

Further on was the ironmongers, Parker, Winder & Achurch. This was a very big shop where I remember lovely companion sets of shovel, brush and poker. They had long slender handles and hung from a stand with a brass figure on top such as a sailing ship like Nelson's Victory. I could imagine one of these sets on our hearth, I could dream, it cost nothing to window shop. I never went into the place though I dearly wanted to.

Nearer to the Hall of Memory, a tiny tobacconist's was squeezed between much bigger buildings with a defiant notice proclaiming, 'The Little Shop With The Big Reputation'. Opposite the Ortho-paedic Hospital was a doll's hospital managed by a cheery, plump lady. I don't know if she performed the operations, but she never had any patients from our part of the world.

You could have your photograph taken at Gaynes's near Saint Emanuel's Church. I remember a large portrait of Godfrey Wynne in the window. From the nearby clothiers you could buy ribbon, underwear, fleecy lined bloomers with elastic at waist and legs, and combinations now known as Long John's which were worn by both sexes. There was also a shop where you could hire or have a costume made for a special occasion, such as appearing with a local amateur dramatic society. This place was like Aladdin's Cave, glittering with precious beads and baubles. I did not know it was all sham, costume jewellery and just looking at it made me happy.

Another shop in a different world from ours lay only two streets from Sheepcote Street. Lee Longlands was, and still is, a very superior furnishing store. I can remember them on two different sites in Broad Street. The first was at the City end before the broadcasting studios were built. Later they moved to the site where Ward's Pork Butchers once stood, and are there still.

Ward's, everybody knew Ward's, just the name brings back the smell of the sawdust they scattered on the floors. Just to look at the hams swinging from rails and tiers of plump, glossy pork pies was a pleasure. They were not cheap; the smallest cost about 9 pence [3.75p] and the party or funeral size were usually only bought by the well off. We did have them occasionally. If someone died and the insurance policy paid out you might have a pork pie and a ham for after the funeral.

One side of Ward's shop sold cooked meats while the other dealt in bacon, sausages, cuts of pork and strange things from inside the pigs. To see the lungs and silky brown livers hanging at the back of the window was like a backcloth in a theatre. Sides of bacon were taken down at the customer's request and sliced to any desired thickness. I would love to stand again in Ward's and be able to have my choice of that lovely array.

While still at school I promised myself that when I went to work I would buy myself one of Ward's pork pies with my first week's money. Some hopes. I couldn't afford to buy even one of the smallest. Our cat did well from Ward's though. Minnie would have a guggle, which was the tube from the pig's throat to its stomach, the lungs or the lites. They cost only a penny and made a couple of good cat meals. Minnie knew the smell of lites and guggle cooking and we could not cool it fast enough for her.

Something that always brought the children running to our street was the cry of, 'The pigs are coming.' The Rec might have been echoing to the shouts of noisy children enjoying themselves, but would suddenly be abandoned as they rushed to the exits, pushing and shoving to get a good look at the pigs. Moving up Sheepcote Street from St Vincent Street, and heading for Ward's, would be a miserable, straggle of a dozen or more pigs.

It was impossible not to look, but it was the most pitiful and shameful sight you ever saw. Even now, over seventy years later, I am filled with pity for those poor animals. They had been walked from a farm said to be in Smethwick, a distance of three miles. They were lead by a cart shaped like a Roman chariot, the horse pulling it moving on at a steady clip-clop, never stopping or slowing. The man in charge was big built with thick arms, and with sleeves rolled to his elbows he patrolled up and down the line of pigs beating the stragglers with a cane. If an exhausted pig collapsed in the road, too tired to move or cry out with pain, the man lashed it harder. If it did not respond he grasped the animal by a front and a back leg and flung it into the cart.

The procession dragged itself slowly to eternity, up Sheepcote Street into Broad Street, turn towards the City then right into Granville Street and right into Tennant Street, to reach Ward's slaughter house. No one questioned what was happening or why such cruelty went on, and if they had nobody would have taken any notice. We followed the saga to its end. Big gates opened and the pigs, suddenly screaming and trying to get out, were herded through to their doom.

It is said that animals can sense death, but it was the smell of that place I never forgot - a nasty, dirty stink which seeped out. I was 8 or 10 years old and the sight of the pigs certainly left its impression on my sense of smell, because the smell of roast pork carried me back to the big gates shutting us 'out' and the pigs 'in'. The nearest we ever got to pork in our house was bacon bones, but even when the chance arose many years later, I could not eat it.

I don't know why I followed the pigs because I didn't enjoy the spectacle. Perhaps it was because just to see a pig was an event, surrounded as we were by bricks and mortar. Pigs meant farms, green grass and trees, but it was in Sheepcote Street that I first saw these lovely animals. It was strange that I never connected the longed for pork pies in Ward's window with the sorry scene of the 'walking pigs'.

Next to Ward's on one corner of Broad Street and Granville Street stood a factory. On the other corner where the Granville Tavern stood was a row of shops, one of which was a greengrocer's, known to us as a vegetable shop. Locals called the Granville the Big House. On the morning it opened the first customer was given free beer, though I don't know how much or for how long. She lived in our street and it was said she had a lovely time.

At Houghton's the butchers, Saturday night was bargain night. The shop would be packed so tight with people that you could hardly lift an arm. Mrs Allen was one of our neighbours who always went to Houghton's for her Sunday joint, and she some-times took me. Being so small I was squashed in, barely able to breath. I could not see what was going on but I could hear the butcher shouting about the bargain he held in his hand and the favour he was doing the crowd. He was not selling the meat, he was giving it away. 'Come on ladies. Ya know a bargain when ya sees one. The quicker this lot is sold the sooner we can all goo 'ome to ower beds'.

These were the days before widespread refrigeration, so all food, and especially fish and meat, had to be sold on Saturday because by Monday it would not be fit to eat. The customers knew all this, and that the longer they held back from buying the more the butcher would reduce his prices. Packed like sardines from counter to walls, those people were not standing there for fun.

Local people were old hands at the game of bargain hunting because they did it every Saturday night, if not at Houghton's then perhaps at Steve's shop in Ryland Street. Only when the right price was called, a half dozen or more hands were raised and a number of voices called out, 'Here.', was the bargain sealed.

Our Mom did not believe in this Saturday night ritual. For one thing, she wanted to go out and leave me to look after Florrie. 'Anyway,' she would say, 'It's all bleeding 'cag-mag' they sell down there - I wouldn't beg the stuff'. 'Cag-mag' described anything not quite up to standard including food, and especially meat. It was always said with a grimace. Cag-mag or not, appetising smells wafted from the Allen's house every day of the week.

The Crown pub in Broad Street still stands and has recently been glorified. Next door there used to be a brewery, and opposite was a small pub called the Hen & Chickens, not an imposing place.

One of the most memorable places was the Prince of Wales Theatre. As a little girl I used to stand outside the glass doors watching ladies and gentlemen in furs and finery meeting their friends. I never dreamed that one day I would join them, actually go inside the Prince of Wales and see for myself the mirrors reflecting the light of hundreds of brilliant electric bulbs.

I can still feel the thrill of my first and last visit to the Prince of Wales, of sitting in a red plush seat amongst packed tiers of people. No longer did I have to look out for the doorman to shoo me away, I had a ticket and the door had been opened for me to enter. There was one surprise, I can't call it a disappointment. I had imagined the auditorium as much bigger than it was. What a night. There were happy, excited children, moms and dads trying to calm them down, bags of sweets being crackled, coats being pushed under seats, and people trying to find seats - 'Excuse me, you're in the wrong row'. But I had the right seat, and although I was then a married woman, I was as excited as any of them when the orchestra started to play, the lights dimmed and the curtain began to rise.

Hitler played a large part in the redevelopment of Broad Street, and to the list of buildings which he destroyed the City Council added others which did not fit with their ideas. It all cost us a great deal of old Birmingham, some of which might have been preserved, like the Crown. But places like the Prince of Wales still live in the memories of us who spent happy hours there.

This poster came a little before Helen's time, but the theatre had probably not changed much when she saw it. Her only visit was in the early 1940s shortly before it was bombed.

Courtesy of Birmigham Housing Education Initiative

Sherborne Street

Some time in 1929 news got round that our houses in Sheepcote Street were going to be demolished. This caused a tremendous stir. Houses were where you were born and died, two or three generations would live in the same little place. You stayed because you had always lived there, despite the conditions. It was 'home'. To be told that you had to move out and find somewhere else to live was strange and shocking. We had our little differences with neighbours but not enough to cause a war.

So off we set one day, Mom, Florrie and 12 year old me. There were no empty houses nearby so we went exploring around Saint Vincent Street. We walked along Great Tindal Street and stopped to look at a big building on the other side. It had been a pub but was now let off as single rooms. Some rooms were 'furnished' and known locally as 'furnished wacks'. As we stood looking a window opened and a head appeared, then smaller heads popped out and called to us from across the road. In no time all the windows were alive with heads, all come to look at us looking at them. I was quite upset and hated the whole scene. It was a dilapidated, dirty, overcrowded hovel.

We walked on and Mom remarked, 'They're only 2/6d a week.' The rent for our house was 4/8d. [15p and 23.5p] For such a saving we could have a breast of lamb and a rabbit, vegetables, enough food for three days if we filled up with bread. But I pleaded, 'Oh no, don't let's live there.' We didn't, we found another bug ridden back to back house around the corner.

How we found the house in Sherborne Street was being vacated I don't know. The door of No. 4/66 was opened by a child with fair, curly hair aged 4 or 5 years. Inside was a scene of poverty and neglect. A woman sat in a chair crowded by several small children who were all in a state of being undressed, and all smiling and happy. She was not very old but we learnt that she could no longer get about because of her 'rheumatics'. She and the children were having to go away because she could not look after them.

Because we had found a house ourselves, we were given £5 by the agents of the Sheepcote Street property. Mom was getting £1 12 shillings [£1.60] each week for the three of us, so £5 was a wonderful bonus. Then the agent for the Sherborne Street house demanded £5 for the key. Extracting 'key money' was one reason that so many people lived as lodgers in a shared house.

The house was the usual type - a living room, a larder, a space under the stairs where you kept the coal, a shelf for cooking utensils (in our case a couple of saucepans and a colander) and a little window to let in some light.

The window was usually left open to air the place, but on one occasion Mom had forgotten the remains of the 'beeve's' heart (cow's heart). It must have smelt good because a cat got in through the little window and our dinner went out.

It was only when we moved in that we had a proper look at the bedroom and the attic where the children had slept. It soon appeared that they had never had a chamber pot. Investigating why a floorboard was missing, I found the cavity littered with faeces. Those children could not go out into the cold night, so they had created their own lavatory, and it was me that had to clear it out.

Another shock was in store for us because the rooms came complete with bed bugs. This was awful because after they had been on your body they left a mark. To go to school or work with the telltale blotches on your face, neck or arms was an embarrassment, you could feel people moving away from you.

During the day these pests retreated into the brick walls, cosy and well fed. At night they emerged as you slept to gorge on your blood. Having spent much of the night catching and killing as many as you could, you would be tired next day until you went back to bed. But the bugs were not tired, they had spent a restful day under the plaster, and so the cycle went on.

The only way the bugs could be held in check was by closing the door and window, blocking up the chimney and placing a chemical in the room. Fumes would then permeate the room and kill a lot of them. Even so, there were another lot that got away by burrowing through the wall to your neighbour's rooms. With three or four hosts to choose from in these clusters of houses, the bugs had a good and lengthy life. You would be free of the pests until the neighbour at the back or either side of you decided they had lost enough sleep, and that it was time they did some 'stoving', as the practice was known.

We were unlucky in our choice of house because these little places could be made very comfortable. The homes of our neighbours and friends were spotlessly clean, with shining blackleaded fire grates complete with a brass fender and fire irons. A black kettle would sing on the hob and the mantlepiece would be fringed with a deep, bobble edged strip of chenille. The better off families would have a velvet cloth on their table. No one had much furniture because there was only room for the bare necessities.

The other facilities in Sherbourne Street were much the same as in Sheepcote Street. In the yard was a similar block of lavatories and brew house, but here there was a little fenced plot of land before each house called a 'garden'.

Now I had a dream of a house with check curtains at the kitchen window and a little garden. I remember standing on the rock hard clay of our newly acquired estate with the idea of digging it up to plant flowers. So where to start? Digging came first, I knew that much, but I knew nothing at all about spades and forks and gardening tools. Spades and shovels could be seen in Parker, Winder & Achurch's window in Broad Street, but I associated them only with navvies digging up the street. From the drawer in our kitchen table I drew the big fork and went out to study the job. My first futile stabs at the ground convinced me that it would need tons of topsoil to plant anything, so my garden ambition was abandoned.

The nearest we came to gardening was our window box where Mom grew smashing sweet peas. Sweet peas grow tall, so to keep them upright we tied a string around them and fastened it to a nail hammered into the window frame. Half a dozen plants in the window make a pretty sight, even if they keep light from your room.

Some gardens in our yard did grow flowers, and they certainly added colour to drab surroundings. The Harpers' who lived in the top house did well, and on sunny days they added their parrot in a cage. He was colourful, greener than anything that grew there, but noisy. It was no good thinking of having a doze among your begonias when he was out.

That bird would shriek and whistle and recite his party piece which was, 'Does your mother want a rabbit?' The answer was, 'Sell her one for ninepence.' Heard the first time it was very funny. It would even make you laugh after, say, half a dozen times. But if the bird was outside for a couple of hours you felt like asking it to extend its repertoire. At this time in the 1930s there was a disease among parrots that worried owners, pet shops and menageries because not only birds were dying, human beings could catch it. I have no idea of exactly what happened to the Harper's bird, but quite suddenly he ceased his warblings.

Soon after we moved into the house we received an official looking printed envelope. Never getting letters from any source made it puzzling. and the only thing to do was open it, which was my job. It was certainly official and from a department of the City Council we had never heard of. Why did it always have to be me that brought the bad news? Mom could have asked a neighbour to read it for her and she might have kept her temper in check.

This time it was the Health Department turning the screw. The occupant of No. 4/66 Sherborne Street was informed that if the house was not cleaned up by such and such a date, proceedings would be brought against said occupant.

Our Mom blew her fuse, and with some reason. We had been in the house only a few days. The children of the previous occupants had been taken into one of the Council children's homes where they would probably stay until they were old enough to earn a living. Their father had failed to help his invalid wife and been sent to prison for neglecting his family.

Get through it we did, but Mom's health was suffering and her eyesight deteriorating. She no longer went to the Eye Hospital or the Ear, Nose & Throat for treatment because there was no more they could do. Mom was registered blind with no hope of recovery.

One day a rumour went round the yard that our houses were to have 'the gas' installed. That caused a great stir, but then we were told water was being laid on too. What had we done to deserve such gifts? No more fetching lamp oil (paraffin) in a bottle, no trimming of lamp wicks and an end to the dangerous practice of seeing your way to bed with a lighted lamp. This had been the cause of many deaths.

The day work started the place was busier than a beehive with comings and goings, the fetching of picks and shovels and examining the yard to decide where to make the first strike. A channel was dug close to the fronts of the houses in which to lay the main gas pipe. This was fine, so long as you could see where you were stepping and could cross to make a footfall by the garden palings.

One Saturday morning some friends called round to say they were going to the swimming baths in Monument Road, and could I join them. To go to the baths meant that I needed money, 3d [1.25p]. I asked Mom if I could I go and was promptly told no. I pleaded with her to give me the 3 pence. Perhaps my pleadings went on for too long or her temper that day was short. I had placed myself carefully beneath a picture of Tommy which hung on the wall near the door. Mon would not throw anything at me here in case she missed and hit the picture. However, she suddenly jumped up and made to grab me. I turned and flew, skipping over the gas pipe trench and racing off down the yard like a whippet. At a safe distance I turned, and to my horror saw that Mom had fallen into the trench. I ran away.

To run away from home in those days was not an easy thing to do. Boys stood a better chance than girls because they could lie about their age and join the army, which lots did. My father joined the Gloucester Regiment when he was only 13.

That day I walked the streets crying a lot, utterly miserable and afraid to face my mother. I knew the beating that was in store for me and did not want to see her again, ever. One of the Bishop sisters had come with me and I confided my plan to her, I would put myself away in a children's home. But where to go, I had no idea. My brother Ted was put into a home so who better to approach than the people who had done it. We set off for the Oratory in Hagley Road, only to find it locked up. I knocked and knocked on the heavy timber door but no one seemed to hear. It was strange those doors being closed because they were so often open.

I had nothing to eat or drink all day. The streets grew quieter as the day wore on, Nancy, or was it Ada, left me and I was on my own. I don't know how long I sat on the Oratory steps before realising that there was no alternative but to go home and face the music. I was in abject misery as I made my way back, feeling quite alone and not caring what Mom did to me. As soon as possible I would leave home, although that was not to be for another two years. When I reached home my mother was sitting by the fire. She looked up but never moved or said a word, so I made my exit while the going was good and went straight to bed.

Harborne

Gas was fitted into the houses in Sherborne Street in 1930. We were there while the mains were laid, but this caused subsidence. Scaffolding was erected to preserve the houses from total collapse, but the doors and windows had a drunken, lopsided look. The main door would not close, it just leaned against the frame so that anyone could move it aside to get in. Somebody did.

One night I lay in bed reading by the light of a bedside candle and ignoring the noise from the Childs's next door. They were having a 'bit of a party', not a proper party with food, just drinking and being noisy. For a change my mother was not among the revellers. I think this was because she had been removed from one such gathering for making a nuisance of herself.

Mother was asleep in a small bed under the window while I was in the big bed with Florrie. Suddenly I heard a sound quite unconnected with the row from the Childs's. I put my book down and listened, too frightened to move. A stair creaked. I sat up and looked at the door, terrified. Slowly, the door started to open and a hand appeared. I screamed and jumped over to my mother's bed, shouting and crying that there was someone in the house. She got up, threw up the sash window, and the two of us made enough noise to rouse the neighbours.

Holding a trembling candle we made our way downstairs. The paraffin lamp was lit but there was really no need to look around to see if anything had been stolen. We could list our treasures on a postage stamp: one pair of red glass vases twined around by black snakes.

The neighbours answering our distress call looked around for the intruder but eventually decided he had gone. After the commotion our midnight visitor was unlikely to call again, so we trooped back upstairs to bed.

Next morning we got up and went for some coal, which was kept under the stairs and reached from the pantry. Whoever had been in the house had mistaken our coal hole for a lavatory, and our Mom, groping for pieces of coal, had put her hands in the mess. Her comments were unprintable.

After some discussion with Mrs Childs about her guests it came out that one man had been missing from the party for a while. He had apparently gone outside for a breath of fresh air but hurriedly returned when the shouting started. His name was Tommy Raison, a coal man. We knew the family. Tommy's sister Martha used to visit us with her baby. Tommy was unmarried and I never knew where he lived, but he was a friend of Mother's.

Perhaps as a result of this incident, but more likely because of the subsidence, the powers decided to move us to Wood-house Road, Harborne. I remember the bathroom, all lovely and white and smelling of fresh paint.

It was not only our house though, we were sharing with the Childs's. They had the ground floor rooms while we three lived in a small room upstairs. It was not a very good arrangement. We were cramped and had to cook on a small bedroom fire.

As neighbours we were on good terms with the Childs's, but living under the same roof was different. We would be sitting quietly when they would suddenly give our door a banging and shout abuse. This happened again and again until we moved back to Sherborne Street. Whatever sharing agreement had been made, the Childs's wanted us out.

Harbourne was in a different world from Ladywood. Down Tennel Lane were farms, orchards and a wood, known as Tom Knocker's Wood. There was a pool with frogs and I went scrumping for pears with other children. On one expedition I fell out of a tree and the pears gave me stomach ache. It was fun while it lasted if you could outrun the dogs that the farmer set on us. I loved walking by lovely green hedges instead of brick walls. In Harborne you could see the sky, it was amazing how much there was, and all around there was space and good air.

If all this was wonderful, the distance to my temporary school in South Road, Harborne was a serious problem. By bus the trip was easy but usually I hadn't got the fare. Fear of being late kept me in tension all through the journey. I did not know what you might be punished for at that school and I did not want to.

We moved back to Sherborne Street after about three months but the Childs's stayed in Woodhouse Road. Mom had something in mind for them when they did return; somehow she had unearthed the knowledge that they were not Mr & Mrs.

The Education

One day we received a letter from the Education Department. It told Mother that Florrie was not doing as well as she should at St Barnabas's School. It had been decided, the letter did not say by whom, that she should attend a 'Special School' in Horse Fair more suited to her needs.

Conformity was then the order of the day. You had to do as everyone else did or you were odd, or funny, 'not like us'. You held a pen or pencil in your right hand, You held a knife or scissors in your right hand. When you picked up a book or a cup it had to be with your right hand, not your left. But for Florrie her right hand was the wrong hand because she was left handed. At school she was not allowed to hold her pen in her left hand and had been smacked for it, though what she wrote was perfectly legible. Not surprisingly, she made no progress and never did become very good at writing. Florrie could read well enough but never had the desire for it.

Mother was more than put out by the Department's letter, she exploded, ranted and raved about what she was going to do to 'them'. I set off to school with Florrie as usual; I never went far without her. The morning lessons passed. At midday we went home to dinner, then returned to school. Mother made no reference to the letter which had thrown her into such a rage. She seemed calm and quiet and her face was stony.

Just after 2.00pm when lessons had started, there was a loud knocking on the school door. Someone answered it, then fetched the headmistress, who closed the door behind her. We all got our heads down again and the lesson started, but over the teachers' voices we could hear another sound, rising in volume and loud enough to distract us. We lifted our heads, looked at one another and wondered whose Mom or Dad was complaining about their child being caned or kept back after school. It did not concern me though; our Mom could not see well enough to get to school.

The shouting went on and we were enjoying it when the headmistress's head appeared round the door, and she called my name. I could not believe it when I saw Mom standing on the landing. 'Take your Mother home' I was told, 'Take her home.' The headmistress had not met Mom before, but she would never forget her. That quietly spoken, educated lady was only trying to say that she had nothing to do with Florrie being sent to a Special School, and in any case, it was for Florrie's good. But Mom had not yet said all she had to say and the poor headmistress had more words flung at her before I could get Mom to the stairs.

One of the teachers came out to help the headmistress. It made no difference because Mother could not see her. I was pulling at Mom's arm but she threw it off as I cried and pleaded. She would not stop until she had released her pent up venom, then I was able to guide her to the stairs where she put her foot on the first step. Here she turned and found further words to insult the headmistress and teachers, keeping up the tirade all the way down the stairs. Only when we stepped through the door into Ledsham Street did it seem that the battle was over. I guided Mom safely home but never discovered how she found her way to the school.

She was tenacious, my mother. She was going to fight 'them' all the way. They were not going to do as they liked with her children a second time, after Ted had been sent to Canada.

Mom did not really have any chance of winning a battle with the Education Department with no one to advise her. Even so, she put her plan into action the next day. We were kept from St Barnabas's and during the morning went up to St John's School in Wood Street. There the headmistress seemed willing to take Florrie into the school and noted her particulars, but nothing was said about the Special School.

I went back to school as usual the next day but Florrie stayed at home until we had news that she could move to St John's. That news never came but the School Board Man did, to visit my headmistress. I was summoned to her desk and the interview was short. First question - did I know a girl named Florence Mason. I did not. Second question - what was my sister's name. 'Florence May Smith, Sir', I replied. The headmistress's face did not move and the School Board Man shot her a knowing look. The headmistress of St John's had heard my sister's name as Mason for May Smith.

Mom did not win her battle but she gave a tough response, and I knew that the teachers at St Barnabas's would not forget her. I wonder whether she gave the impression of a loving, caring mother fighting for her child? I am sure some people had their grievances

93

listened to politely and were given sugary answers while official wheels were set in motion against them. With us authority could not be bothered and treated us like imbeciles.

As it turned out Mother need not have been upset about the Special School because Florrie was very happy there. She passed her examination and was able to leave school at the same age as everyone else, which was 14.

'The Old Steam Clock'

Ron (Smudge) Smith's wonderful, cartoon style painting shows the bustling corner of Morville Street and Sherbourn Street, perhaps in the early 1930s. There is every form of life, from carthorses to mice, window cleaners to pigtailed schoolgirls. Most of the carts and lorries explain themselves, but can you work out what is on the snorty looking lorry on the right? The Old Steam Clock was was the name of the pub but no one seems to know why.

To Work

As Florrie settled in her new 'special' school in the Horse Fair, Mom also moved me to another school. This which was in Piggot Street just off Bath Row and opposite the Queen's Hospital and Davenport's Brewery.

The school building was new in 1931, with large airy rooms and vast, high windows which let in plenty of light. There were fewer children in each class than at St Barnabas's and we had boys and girls together. The headmaster was Mr English. When Mom took me to be enrolled we went into his study and she was given a chair to sit on. I can't remember what was said but I can remember how soft spoken and kindly he was. I was not long at the school but I was happy, and did quite well in my exams, coming second in the class.

During August of that year I went camping with the Birmingham Boys and Girls Union for a week on Lord Atherstone's estate at Penkridge, Staffordshire. School started again at the beginning of September but shortly afterwards I fell ill. This kept me off school until December, by which time I was old enough to leave.

This illness was very painful. I had lumps and swellings behind my knees which hampered my walking, more on the back of my neck, and the glands in my throat and behind my ears were inflamed. I saw a doctor at the Dispensary in Monument Road who diagnosed some form of rheumatism. He prescribed a treatment I will never forget. I had to paint iodine inside of my mouth and as far down my throat as I could reach. For this operation I was given a long handled brush with the head set at an angle. It was not easy and made me retch at first, but I had to get over that.

When I was well enough I went to Wassal Grove Convalescent Home in Hagley for a fortnight. This was not far from what was then the Gipsy's Tent public house, now The Badger's Set. It was a lovely house with gardens full of trees. When I arrived I weighed 5 stones 4 ounces. At the end of my stay I was 5 stones 4 pounds, the result of ample quantities of good food.

The days at Wassall Grove were heaven, but not the nights. I dreaded going to bed because we could hear trains on the line from Birmingham to Kidderminster. Whenever I heard a whistle it took me back to Sheepcote Street on the night Tommy went missing. I would stand looking out of the window into the night to see if I could see the train, but never did. That whistle sent a chill through me, and I still feel the same when I remember it.

A school friend brought my School Leaving Certificate, or 'character' as it was known. This document was very important when applying for a job, and as it turned out, especially for me. The box marked 'Attendance' said 'Poor', which of course it was. For English it said 'Good'. I can't remember any other comments except that at the bottom of the certificate the 'Headmaster's Report' read, 'She is an honest, reliable girl. Applies herself willingly to work. Is honest and truthful.' I wish I still had that document.

The weight I had gained during my convalescence was soon lost when I started work after Christmas 1931. Mother took me job hunting. The first place she chose was the first we came to in Cumberland Street. I stood on the step and knocked at the door. There was no answer so I knocked again harder. After a while the door opened to reveal a sour looking man who eyed us critically and rapped, 'Wha cha wont?'. It was pure, unadulterated Brummagem, and he was so softly spoken I almost fell of the step.

I got off his step and stood beside Mom, leaving her to explain why we had brought him to the door. She asked him in a very civil manner, remarkably civil for her, whether they were setting any girls on? Without moving a muscle he fixed his eyes on me and in a most offensive way said, 'Oo 'er? 'Er looks us if er's gonna drop down dead eny minute'. Then he took a step back and slammed the door.

I thanked my lucky stars there were no vacancies. I was in the pink of condition after my holiday, but obviously not robust enough for the work they did at that place. Next Mom took me to Jones & Berkley in Bath Row. I can't think why because it was a long walk from where we lived. Yes, we were told, they did have a vacancy and I could start next day.

It was decided I should go on the tram, which I did for a few days. I asked for a half fare and got it, though the conductor must have known I was not going to school at 8 o'clock in the morning. By going half fare I saved a penny [.4p] on each trip, and since I made four journeys each day it was a good saving. It took longer, but soon I started walking to work, meeting some of the girls I worked with and chatting as we went along.

I never knew what product was made by Jones & Berkeley. They told me what to do and the quicker I did it the better. I worked a hand press. You had to get a rhythm but I soon learned to lean back as I pulled the handle round to the front of me. If you didn't you gave yourself a nasty bang on the side of the head. The first and only time this happened I wondered who had delivered the blow.

A spiral staircase lead from the room where we worked to the floor above, the first I had ever seen. I would have liked to have climbed it but never did.

For what reason I don't know, but only weeks after starting the job Mother told me one Friday that I was not going to work there any longer. You didn't ask my mother questions and I was happy enough to have a day off. During the afternoon we set off for Jones & Berkeley to collect my wages of between 9 and 10 shillings for a 48 hour week [45p to 50p]. With the pay packet in her hands, Mom started a tirade. She was taking away one of their 'slaves', their workers were like navvies and they didn't need girls, but donkeys. In fact, I had never complained about the job because I liked it.

I had to get another job quickly. The 5 shillings each week Mom had for me was stopped when I left school. This left her the 10 shillings widow's pension and 2 shillings and 6 pence for Florrie. [25p, 50p and 15p] Without telling Mom, I set off for Reeves's in the Crescent behind Cambridge Street. I had heard Mom mention the place because she worked there as a young girl. Another thing in its favour was that it was not far to walk. I was taken on by the gaffer and went jubilantly home. Mom was not at all happy, she said they were a rough lot who worked there. Anyway, I had cast the die and set off next morning, mingling with the rest of the employed.

The gaffer at Reeves's was Mr Timmins and he had complete control. He was the manager, tool setter, repairer, maintainer, work scheduler, progress chaser, orderer of supplies, organiser of despatches, discipliarian and wage payer. Mr Timmins was everywhere, the hand presses, the pickling shop, the polishing shop or the switch room. He started the motor which set the machines in motion at 8 o'clock in the morning and switched it off at precisely 5.30 when we all poured out.

Mr Timmins had been at Reeves's when Mom worked there twenty years before, in fact he worked there for over sixty years. It was his first and only job, and when he died the

Evening Mail ran it. He was a good boss and his loyalty
to Reeves's was reflected in the workers' loyalty to him.
Mr Timmins spoke little and was always Mister. I once
heard him called Bill, but such familiarity would not
have been accepted from younger workers.

The firm made many things including components for the
electrical trade, so said the sign on the roof. There were
light switches with brass covers, holders for light bulbs and
dozens of bits and pieces. You would not expect coffin nails
to be part of their output, but I pierced thousands of them.

Alf the stamper gave the nails their shape in thin brass, then I
pierced a series of very small holes round the rim as a decoration. I never saw them in their finished state. After Alf died
we had a big order for coffin nails and someone said that the
old chap was doing a bit of canvassing in the kingdom on high.

There were two stampers, old Alf and his much younger mate.
They stood in a gully in the floor. Attached to the stamp was
a rope which went up and over a beam, while the other end hung
below the machine and had a loop through which the worker put
his foot. The stamper would pull the rope down with right foot,
place the job on the bed and release the rope, allowing the stamp
to fall. It came down with such a thud. Imagine doing that job
eight and a half hours a day for five and a half days each week.

At the age of 14, I was the youngest person working at Reevses's
and the dog's body. It did not matter to me what job I was given
because none of it was heavy or dirty, and I would happily move
from one to another at any time.

Reevses's building was not very large and just two storeys high,
but it was peculiar in that one workroom was a large balcony which
ran round the walls. This was where coffin nails were pierced and
bulb holders made, along with those little gadgets on curtain rings
from which you hang the hooks.

I did not like working on the balcony because it was cold and
you would be sitting there hour after hour. On one occasion Mr
Timmins brought a box of hot sawdust for me to put my feet in,
and sometimes he would send me to other departments to thaw.

One such time he sent me to the burnishing shop to dry out
switch covers. That was lovely and warm. The covers were
put into a riddle which was immersed into a box of hot sawdust and then shaken until all the sawdust had fallen back.

The knack of this job was to move the riddle to and fro while keeping the rest of your body still. Try it. There were half a dozen people on the job and they all stopped work to watch me. I felt like a jelly on a plate. Sawdust flew off the riddle but so did the covers I was supposed to be drying. One of the ladies gave me a demonstration. She had been at the job for years and to me seemed elderly, but she was an expert and made it look so simple. I took a little time to master that job because I did not want to go back to that balcony too soon.

The rough side of work at Reeves's was a small dark room on the ground floor where brass curtain rings about six inches in diameter were threaded onto narrow strips of brass ready for annealing. This was a dirty job which I was not asked to do often.

I can't remember seeing anyone smoking at work but there were snuff takers, and it only took a second to have a secret pinch. The most disgusting habit, and in all my life I only knew one man who did it, was chewing tobacco. Chewing the plug was not offensive, but he did not swallow the juice, he ejected it up the wall where he was working, leaving dark brown stains. I could not do anything about it and when I was in the burnishing shop I had to fetch his work along with the rest, but I felt sick just looking at his horrible corner.

All the heavy machinery was on the ground floor with big power presses making a thump, thump, thump hour after hour. Mary operated one of them and I remember her singing a popular song of the time, 'Carolina Moon', which might have helped pass the time and take her mind off the noise. I guessed Mary's age to be 18.

One morning the big presses suddenly stopped their thumping. Everywhere there was silence and the workers stopped talking. I did not understand it until later, when someone told me, very quietly, that poor Mary had had an serious accident on her machine and lost some of her fingers. That episode put me in fear of those big, black monsters, and I never worked on them.

My favourite job was working in the shop where the light switches were assembled. It was a light, clean room shut off from the rest. The door closed after each person, so no noise penetrated and it had a comforting feeling. 'Ladies' worked in the switch room, they were more mature than the other girls. There was no larking or laughing or taking a rise out of the beginner.

It was easy to get mixed up between the 'things' in the little box on my left and the near identical 'things' from the box on the other side. When I dipped into the wrong box the woman sitting beside me would let me make my mistake, but then point out the right box without raising her voice.

The work required concentration and dexterity. The screw drivers were difficult to handle, especially the long ones on which you placed a little nut brass to hold down the contacts you had just assembled in the correct order ready to slip down a small screw. The next operation was a tricky one, with thumb and little finger firmly holding the base of the switch, you held down the contacts with the index and third finger of your left hand. Reversing your hand so that the back of the switch faced you, you placed the nut over the protruding screws.

It was difficult to learn because one false move could mess up the whole operation. But there would be smiles and words of encouragement from the experts and someone would start singing a song from a show or film appearing in town, and so to themes from The Desert Song or The Student Prince, I would begin to assemble the switch again, not in the least flustered or embarrassed. After a day or two I mastered the art. The switch room at Reeves's was like being in heaven.

Apart from proper working accidents there were also the silly, uneccessary ones that happen in every workplace. One Saturday morning Annie Beddows was chasing me out of the polishing shop and I ran through a glass panelled door, swinging it shut behind me. In trying to stop it closing the poor girl put her arm through a pane. Blood poured from the gash. Somebody wrapped it up and I went with her to the Midland Hospital in Easy Row where she had seven stitches. That hospital and the rest of Easy Row were all demolished in the 1950s and 60s.

Most of the jobs I did at Reeves's were light, easy and not at all life threatening, but there was a process on the porcelain switch bases which was quite dangerous. Two small holes had to be filled with hot wax. This was melted in a pot which stood on a gas ring. I sat at the bench in front of the pot and turned on a tap which released a spot of hot wax into each hole. What would the consequences have been if that pot had been knocked over? Nobody thought twice about the waxing and I enjoyed it because I was warm. In any case, you just got on with whatever you were given because any work was better than none.

Before going to work I would have a piece of bread and marg and a cup of tea, and take 2 pence to buy something for my dinner. There was a cook shop in Camden Street where you could get a good slice of spotted dick pudding for 2 pence. By the time you had carried it up King Edwards Road and round the Crescent to Reeves's it had cooled down, but this made no difference. Hot or cold it was 'feeding' and 'stuck to 'ya ribs' all afternoon.

I used to run errands for anyone who had nothing for their dinner and usually went to a small shop in Loveday Street where you could get biscuits and chocolate. Coming back from one of these errands I stopped to watch two men setting ladders against one of the old houses. They were a few feet apart and each man began to climb hauling up a signboard. I forgot all about the girl at Reeves's waiting for her biscuits. When the sign was in place, it read 'Crescent Theatre'. This left me no wiser and I probably got a telling off for dawdling, but I can claim to have been at the birth of that famous theatre in early 1932.

Timekeeping at work was vital. If your working day started at 8 o'clock you were expected to be sitting at your place ready for the machinery to start. Everything came to life at that precise second. One morning I was a bit late, so I ran from the house and halfway down the yard, where I fell. My knee was covered in blood so I took myself to the Queen's Hospital where my knee was cleaned, bandaged and put in a splint, after which I limped to work.

The main entrance that the workers used was locked, so I banged on the warehouse door. The tall, thin warehouse lad opened it and looked a me with a huge grin. It wasn't every day that a casualty knocked on his door and it brightened things up.

He came to the edge of the loading bay, took hold of my hands and hauled me up. Having one stiff leg made it quite difficult. I went in search of Mr Timmins who let me stay. If he had sent me home I would have been short in my pay packet and had Mom's tongue to deal with as well as my knee.

Life was getting easier. There were no more tannings, and the odd punch, when Mom could land one, just bounced off. I was fancying myself, feeling my feet, growing up, and with money in my pocket. I grew loud and cheeky, with no more respect for my mother than she had ever shown me, but loving and protective of my little sister. Florrie had not got my temperament and was too afraid of her mother.

There were still the household errands to be run and Florrie took on some of the jobs when she got home from school, but I was still the one who fetched the coal from the wharf.

When we lived in Sheepcote Street we got it from the wharf in Oozells Street North. The barrows were built to withstand the coal falling from the scales, and were so heavy that we only bought a quarter hundredweight at a time because this was all I could push. Our nearest coal yard to Sherborne Street was in Browning Street, which was better because there were no inclines.

You can't compare a 14 year old of today with a 14 year old of the 1920s and 30s. We were held back, not encouraged to mature and not allowed opinions. If you did say what you thought about something you would be accused of trying to 'run the show', 'too big for ya boots', and so on. But my Friday wage packet was proof enough of my ability to earn a living. As a worker I no longer wanted to be treated like a schoolgirl and thought I should be given more freedom to go out at night. I was grown up enough to work 48 1/2 hours but had to pay it all to mother, and if I asked for 4d to go to the pictures during the week I knew what the answer would be.

Katie Mortimer was going to see Maurice Chevalier. He was very popular and nearly every man who had fought in France seemed to have been with Maurice in the trenches. He was in a singing and dancing extravaganza called The Love Parade. The photos outside the Ledsam Picture House showed the dancing girls in their beautiful costumes surrounding the great man, and he leaning on a cane with his straw boater cocked over one eye. I could hear him singing 'You are my ideal - My Love Parade', a song I had heard on Mom's radio headphones. I left Katie outside the 'blood tub' (cinema) still chewing her rock. She never, ever, gave me any.

Katie was not my mother's favourite. One night when I said that I was going out with her Mother said 'Then you can't go out'. I remember sitting on the bow bawling my eyes out and accusing my mother of not wanting me to do anything or go anywhere. We lived further from the library now and I could not just pop out for a book, so I went to bed.

I had been working at Reeves's for about fifteen months and enjoying it, then coming home one Saturday morning Katie met me in the street. 'I'm coming to work at your place on Monday', she said. I froze.

In those days of high unemployment there was always somebody to step into your shoes and you never 'spoke' for a friend. To get them a job where you worked was to lose yours. What should I do? Keep the news to myself, say nothing, and hope my mother did not find out, because if she did she would accuse me of 'speaking' for Katie and putting my own job at stake.

Since Katie lived only in the next yard Mom was sure to find out, so I decided to tell her myself. I found Mom sitting by the fire and told her what Katie had said, adding hastily before she had time to breathe, 'I didn't speak for her, so I'm not going back to Reeves's any more. I'll get another job.' Dear God, to be so absolutely dominated to the point of having my life made a misery, leaving a job I enjoyed, and worst of all, leaving friends that I might never see again.

I had suffered bruises. Some had showed, others were cover-ed by clothes, like the gash on my hip when Mom threw a bottle at me, or when she beat me on the back with a broom handle. Those wounds heal, but living in a stressful situation day after day leaves its mark too. After years it takes root, leaving memories so bitter that at times, like now as I write it all down, I want to scream, Why? Perhaps it was because I was there, the only target for her hurts and spite. I should not have been there because I only added to her grief over losing Tommy. I was still only 15 years old, going on 50.

On Monday morning I set off to find a new job. Gran had once worked in the jewellery quarter so I thought I might give it a try. I was seeing pretty things instead of dreary old coffin nails. I had not taken distance into account and it was long walk. After knocking on a few doors asking if they wanted any girls, I began to think that business was not too brisk in that area. Retracing my steps up Broad Street I remembered that Rosy Goode worked at Collins's in Cumberland Street, which was much nearer home. Yes, they did need a girl, but what experience did I have? I told of the work I had been doing, unskilled but certainly varied. 'Right, start in the morning, 8 sharp,' I was told.

The news that I had got another job did not make the papers or even cause shouts of joy at 4 back 66 Sherborne Street. Mom asked no questions, such as how much I would be paid or what would I be doing? It was a bit unnerving. She had been quieter lately. Perhaps the ranting and raving had left her because she was a sick woman.

Collins's made hinges, small, medium and large. They came
in two halves which were fitted together and a pin driven down
the centre. Dainty brass hinges were for jewellery boxes, larger
ones were for cupboards and so on. I will not go through Collins's
catalogue except to say that it was a joy assembling the small and
medium hinges, but I hadn't the strength to wield the wooden
mallet for the railway carriage door hinges

Collins's could not be compared to Reeves's. It was noisy, dirty,
and smelly, with many and varied machines. In one small area
there were drilling, countersinking and milling machines and
capstan lathes, all noisy and running at the same time. From
time to time the carriage door hinges were struck mighty blows
by some stronger wench than me. I worked on all these machines
and sometimes went on until 6.30 or 7.00pm, which meant a nice
little pay packet on Friday night.

On Friday nights one of the girls stood outside on the pavement
holding out a tin cup into which we all dropped a penny because
she cleaned the lavatories. There were only two lavatories for
all of us and they were always littered with fag ends and bits
of newspaper. The girl had a nice little racket going because I
would not have known whether they had been cleaned or not.

The workers numbered a dozen or more women, and like the
hinges, they came in different sizes. I was small, but Maggie
Carroll was very small. She had to stand on a box to do some
jobs. She was a fiery person and what she lacked in height
she made up for by assertiveness.

Rosie Goode was always quiet and we got on well together,
but on one occasion Rosie showed that she could hold her own.
Working in the same shop was the niece of one of our former
neighbours, named Nellie. She and Rosie had had a difference
of opinion which suddenly erupted. Nellie was shouting at the
top of her voice, reminding Rosie of her humble beginnings.
Nellie had fared better in that respect. She had never known
what it was like to be hungry. Everyone had stopped work.
Rosie always had a bright colour but was now scarlet. For a
while she let her opponent carry on with her abusive remarks,
then played her ace. 'At least', she said so that everybody
could hear, 'I did have a father.'

Working on the machines with a bit of overtime I was taking
home between 14 and 16 shillings a week, [70p/80p] which
meant more pocket money for me. On a good week I would
have 2 shillings [10p]. Out of this I bought stockings at 6d

[2.5p] to 9d per pair. Pure silk stockings were expensive and out of reach of working girls, so we had hardwearing lisle. They did not ladder and if you had a hole where your shoe rubbed, you darned it. You went on darning holes until you had to buy a new pair, then the old ones would have the much darned feet cut out and the ends stitched up to be worn by your little sister.

After work I would go to Nancy and Ada Bishop's house. We would either hang around the street or go window shopping. One night a week we went to a club on the corner of St Vincent Street and Ledsam Street known as Tenby House. Here we were taught how to embroider and made necklaces, not just threading beads on a string but making fancy patterns.

Our club was affiliated to the Birmingham Boys and Girls Union and in 1931 or 32 it staged a pageant. Hundreds of us assembled one Sunday morning on the stage of the Gaumont Cinema in Steelhouse Lane to rehearse Land of Hope and Glory. We were told when to hold our notes - 'Mother of the free' -2-3-4, 'How shall we extol Thee, Who are born of Thee' - this time holding the note longer. Some of us ran out of breath and were coming up for air before the conductor lowered his baton. There were posters all over the place announcing, 'The Comet is Coming'. 'The Comet' was a printed sheet showing the route the procession would take in the City centre, the clubs involved and the role they played. Our club was halted outside the General Hospital to do a little dance in our pretty frocks, courtesy of B.B.G.U, for the benefit of patients well enough to sit on the outside balconies.

The procession ended at the Kyrle Hall in Sheep Street, headquarters of the BBGU, where a concert was given ending with Land of Hope and Glory. Whenever I hear that stirring music I am back on that stage singing my heart out. We could all say that we had trodden the boards for an hour or so, that was our hour of glory.

One name stands out from that day - Harry Broughton. We stood together singing and must have exchanged names. I never knew where he lived or which club he belonged to and never met him again. But I do know his was the first wartime wedding to take place at St Martin's Church in The Bull Ring. I have a book or two on old Brum and his wedding photograph is in it.

I only worked at Collins's for a month or so before finding myself a job at Saunders's in St Mary's Street near Monument Road. They were one of the many brass founders in Ladywood. The only things I remember working on were called pull rings,

which were screwed to the frame of a sash window so you
could raise and lower it. It was light work and I was getting
better wages on piecework.

Things seemed to be going along quite well. I worked hard but
was happy to do any job asked of me and I liked the people at
Saunders's. They were more mature than at Collins's; most
had been there for years and seemed content with their lot.

One evening I got home from work when Mom asked, 'Would
you like to go into service?' My immediate answer was yes. I
was not told and did I ask where was I going, I just jumped at
the chance. Going into service meant leaving home but I had
no qualms about that. I was 16 and it seemed like an adventure.
I was going away.

On the morning I left home a lady called to collect me. Mom
and me never kissed goodbye. First we went to Lewis's to get
my hair cut, the first time it had been cut by a professional.
From there I was taken to an office in Margaret Street and
given a cup of tea. Next I remember standing on a station
looking at a board saying Barnt Green. A chauffeur walked
up asking if I was Miss Smith? He held open the car door
with a warning to mind my head. I sat in awe as we passed
the beautiful houses, and when we ran down the drive to
Upwood it was the nearest I had ever been to Heaven.

*Upwood, a grand late
Victorian house in the
mixed styles of the
arts and crafts
movement.*

Upwood

'Emmie,' said Margaret the cook, 'You forgot to fill the stove last night, the water's cold and Mrs Gibbons can't have her bath.' I didn't know I had to look after the stove, but Bessie the kitchen maid scurried to get paper and sticks, there was coal in the scuttle and we had it alight in no time. I don't think Mrs Gibbons got her bath that morning, but for the rest of my time at Upwood I never forgot to fill the stove.

The stove was the last job of a long day for a Between Maid, more often called a Tweeny, or dog's body. My day began at 7 o'clock and the first job was to wake cook with a cup of tea at 8.00. Her room was off what used to be a school room. There were stacks of little chairs and a very large and fascinating doll's house. I could have played house for hours, but someone was always wanting Emmie for such and such a job.

Upwood was a real house with real people to be cared for, and I had my place in running it. The family who lived at Upwood included Mrs Gibbons (who missed her bath), who was my employer though I never spoke to her. She was in her 80s and spent a lot of time in her room. On one occasion I came down from the upper floor as Mrs Gibbons was making her way to the staircase leading to the ground floor. Should I go and help her because she was almost blind, or would that be 'forward'? Against my better judgement I stood and watched until she was safely on the stairs.

Mrs Gibbons had a companion, Miss Bowles, a slight lady with a gentle air and kindly smile. She seemed elderly to me, but at 16 anyone over 25 was elderly. Then there were the sisters, Miss Ada and Miss Martha, and their brother Mr John. They all appeared elderly too, dressed in long, sombre clothes.

Miss Martha was the housekeeper and decided what the family would eat. Every morning she came into the kitchen to discuss the day's menu with Cook. Homes of any size were not so well equipped in those days. Having no refrigerator meant that meat and fish were brought in fresh as ordered, so the butcher called every morning.

Milk still came around the streets daily in churns carried on little push carts. In Ladywood you could hear the milk man calling, 'Milk O.' long before he came in sight and you would fetch it in a jug. In Barnt Green things were more discreet.

Mr John, what could I say about him? Not a lot, except that he was a very dour person who never looked happy and seemed to have no household duties.

Miss Ada must have had duties because Upwood was a very large and lovely house which took a lot of organising. I think she took charge of the linen because I often saw her in the room where blankets, sheets and so on were kept. Laundry was put into a large cane basket which was collected weekly, when another was delivered full of wonderful fresh, clean bedclothes, tablecloths and all manner of underwear.

Miss Ada's duties seemed to include inspecting my work, which was mainly helping Cook prepare vegetables, washing up and housework. On one occasion Cook said Midss Ada had comp-lained that I had not cleaned the lavatory. I protested that I had, but Cook told me to flick the cloth over it again and pretend.

I had prepared vegetables at home using a knife, but now I was given a new fangled peeler. It was amazing how the skin came away from the potatoes leaving them a nice shape. I could have done with a peeler at home. Mother used to stand over me as I worked and put her hand into the bowl to feel the peelings. If they were too thick for her liking I would be smacked on the face. On one occasion I had to buy a pound of potatoes with a penny of my own to make up for what I had wasted.

One day, Cook put down a bag and told me to, 'Do these'. I emptied the contents into a bowl to find the oddest shaped things covered in lumps and warts. This was my introduction to artichokes, and my peeler was no use for that job. I was all for cutting off the lumps and making a quick job of it, but an arti-choke without them would be a sorry sight. Later I was given a taste but did not think they were worth the bother.

Other things were new to me as well, such as coffee. I had to grind the beans, producing that delicious smell. It was years before I tasted my first cup of coffee and I was very disapp-ointed. The aroma was the same though, and whenever I see coffee beans being ground I am back in the kitchen at Upwood.

Off the kitchen was a larder where the milk was kept in a large brown earthenware bowl, or crock. After it was filled the milk was left for a while to settle. Then I had to shut myself in the larder 'to keep out the germs', Cook said, and with a spoon skim off the cream and put it into a small silver jug for Mrs Gibbons's first cup of tea. This job needed care because if you dipped the spoon too deep you got milk as well as cream and had to wait until the milk had settled again before you could carry on.

Shut up in that room I had plenty of time to think, and I thought it was not quite fair that the rest of us should have milk that had. been 'milked'. One morning a couple of spoonfuls of cream missed the jug and I had to dip into the milk to top up it up. The cream was wasted on me because I did not like milk and never drank it, but I was curious to know if cream tasted any different. After that Mrs Gibbons had her full ration, and any germs I was carrying because I used the same spoon.

I never knew where Cook or the other two maids came from apart from the fact that they were 'country girls', and that Nellie the housemaid had a brother named Hedley.

Nellie was a cut above Bessie and me. Her job was to wait on the family at meal times and answer the door to visitors. She wore a very smart dark dress with a white apron, a neat head dress of starched white linen and white slip on cuffs, black stockings and lace up shoes. I loved her shoes because they were high heeled, whereas mine were flat and fastened with a buttoned strap.

Nellie had a little kitchen to herself where she prepared afternoon tea for the family. The silver tea and coffee sets were kept here and the more often used china, Nellie duties included cleaning the silver, one of the occasions when she removed her cuffs. She was also generally available for any little jobs the ladies of the house asked to be done.

I had to wear a white cap with a blue dress cum overall, and both were far too big. My flat, button up shoes were too big as well. Completing the ensemble was a rough linen apron worn when I was preparing vegetables, washing dishes or scrubbing the front step. There I was, a pint sized tweeny in quart sized clothes given to me when I arrived.

Two shillings a week [10p] was taken from my wages for wear and tear on these garments. My wages were 8 shillings a week [40p] plus board, food and lodging. After the 2 shilling deduction I didn't have much to squander, but I was still much better off than living at home and working in a factory. I was eating well and often, the environment was worlds better and I still had more money for myself because I had to give less to Mother.

The servants' sitting room at Upwood was a cosy place with a
fire always glowing in the grate. In the evenings there was quiet
conversation to wind down because all of us had a full day. This
was before vacuum cleaners and spray polishes, when carpets were
brushed and furniture was polished with beeswax. The cutlery was
cleaned with a ground pumice powder which was made into a paste
and rubbed on with a damp cloth, then washed and dried. You had
to be careful with the forks or you stabbed yourself.

Every week I had a free half day and a few hours on Sunday after-
noons after the lunch dishes had been washed and the cooking stove
cleaned. I used to go home to see Mom and Florrie in Sherborne Street.

My mother would be wearing headphones to listen to the wireless
set supplied by the RNIB. She had been blind for some time and
could not go out alone, so the radio was a marvellous thing. Mom
got a lot of pleasure from hearing old songs and new ones.

I was never very happy on these visits. Mother would always nag
me about something: where had I been, why hadn't I gone straight
home?, 'I suppose you've been to see your friends before me', on
and on. She also expected me to hand over my wages and I always
gave her some money, but she was never satisfied. To me she just
seemed in her usual bad temper and I did not realise that she was
very ill. I loved getting onto the train back to Barnt Green.

I did not mind walking along Shepley Road in daylight but I was
not so brave in the dark and was always glad to reach the lodge.
This was where Mr Brown lived, the Gibbons's chauffeur. Then
came a short walk down the dark drive to the servant's gate and I
would walk into the kitchen and happiness. The other staff would
be sitting round the fire, and as I entered smiling faces made me
feel wanted. There was always friendly chatter, with Cook
knitting or sewing, until bedtime at 10 o'clock.

Upwood was like a palace after a small terraced house in Ladywood where we lived packed like chickens in a hen house. Whether
they were 'Good Old Days' depended on which side of the tracks
you were born. I did enjoy being in service, the lovely house
surrounded by trees and beautifully kept gardens with a wood
at the back.

One day Bessie was allowed to take me round the grounds and
gardens. I could hardly believe my eyes; flying around the trees
were the prettiest birds I had ever seen, obviously Blue Birds.

110

Until then I had seen only dowdy sparrows and Mr Foxhall's pigeons. These tiny birds made a sweet twittering sound and fluttered gaily through the trees. They had something to sing about; fresh air to breathe, food all around and spacious trees to live in. The poor little 'sparrers' of Ladywood needed a big cough to clear the soot from their little lungs before they could manage a tweet. It was many years before I discovered that my Blue Birds were Blue Tits, and whenever I see them it takes me back again to that garden.

Death of my Mother

I had been at Upwood for about eight weeks, working hard but enjoying every minute. A Tweeny got very little time off so I did not see a lot of my Mom or Florrie. Then in late December 1933 I received a letter telling me that my mother had just come out of hospital and I was needed at home to look after her.

That Christmas of 1933 will be with me always as the worst I can remember. Evelyn Herbert had invited me to their house in Morville Street for Christmas Evening. They were a large family and there was always something going on so I was looking forward to going. Wearing my coat I looked in at the bedroom to say goodbye.

Our Mom sat up in bed with the dejected little figure of Florrie on a chair beside her. The two of them were dimly lit by the gas mantle on the wall, and at that moment I realised how ill Mom really was.

At Evelyn's the door was opened wide with a 'Come in, Come in, Merry Christmas.' Someone pressed a little package into my hand. The room was full of enough Herberts to fill it and they were all happy, teasing and joking. What was Christmas if not a time to celebrate? I opened my present, which was a bottle of Yardley's lavender perfume. Suddenly it was all too much for me, I could not get that bedroom scene out of my mind and I started to cry. Evelyn put her arm round me asking what was the matter? I could only say 'Our Mom is bad.'

In January 1934 my brother, Ted, left the Army and came home from India. He returned to conditions even worse than when he had left seven years before. Mother was ill in bed for eleven weeks. Ted had been home one month and Florrie was a day short of her 11th birthday when Mom died on February 28th.

The morning of my mother's death, Mrs Fisher, who was a nurse, came and sat with me at the bedside. Before she died Mom turned her head towards me, she was totally blind, and said, 'Look after Florrie, won't you?'. I promised I would. A short time later she spoke again, 'Don't leave me, will you, Nellie?', her last words.

That afternoon Florrie cried all the way home from school. The poor little girl was begging me 'Don't put me in a Home, will you? Please don't put me in a Home.' I kept my promises to them both.

Mom had made over her Liverpool Victoria Assurance policy to me months before she died and it paid £48, a fair amount in 1934. From this I paid the funeral expenses to the undertaker and we have put his receipt amongst the pictures along with another from Witton Cemetry. The title deeds of the grave are in my name but I never claimed them.

The cards mention in Blakemore's receipt were known as Death Cards and were given to relatives and friends as a memento. They were 6" x 3" folded white cards edged in black. Printed inside were the name and age of the deceased opposite a verse on the other. On Mom's death card this read: 'God saw her growing weary, The hill too hard to climb, So He gently closed her tired eyes, And said Let Peace Be Thine. At age 46 years.'

Florrie's husband is also buried in Witton Cemetery under a black marble headstone. He lies alone because Florrie made it clear that she did not want to be buried, and we respected that when she died aged 70 on 18th June 1993. My family are in no doubt about my wishes and burying is not among them. I had no say how I entered this world but I am going to leave it in my own style.

While Mom was lying in the house before the funeral, Ted came home one day and produced a coat he had bought for me. I think he was throwing a sprat to catch a mackerel and hoping that I was going to give him mother's insurance money. He didn't know his sister. I had not forgotten writing to him in India asking for money, and the callous reply months later.

Later I did relent a little and gave him £3 to buy a suit for the funeral, but the rest went back where it would be safe for the time being, on Mom's feet in her coffin. After settling the funeral expenses I put the remaining cash in the Post Office.

After Mom's funeral there was nothing left to stay for. I picked up the paper carrier bags holding our few bits of clothing, came down the stairs and went to the box holding the important papers. From it I took what was to me, and certainly to Mother, the most treasured possession - the printed poem given and signed by Annie Chamberlain, Mrs Neville Chamberlain, on 13th September 1924. I also took my parents' marriage lines.

There were a few portraits, probably taken at Gales the Photographers opposite Grey's department store. One of Florrie and I appears on page 60 of this book. It was taken just after Christmas when she was 4 years old and I was 9. Florrie with her blonde hair looked a treat in her red velvet frock. Mine was also velvet but a wishy washy green, which I didn't like

I tucked the treasures in amongst our clothes and we went to the front door. Looking up, I saw Tommy's picture on the wall. It was too big to carry so I took it to Mrs Harper and asked her to keep it until I could collect it? My biggest regret is that I never went back. If anyone has a picture in a black frame of a curly haired little boy standing on a seat, with a death card on either side, that's our Tommy.

From the moment I handed Tommy's photo to Mrs Harper I can remember nothing of the rest of that day. It was a traumatic and anxious time. Leaving Ladywood was a big step and I had the added responsibility of caring for Florrie. I did what I thought was the only thing I could do, and I had her assurance in later life that it was right. I am still not sure - R.I.P Floss.

I am now 81 years old and the story of my life in all its details came flooding out of my mind as I wrote it down. All the pain is still there. It is incredible that I have such vivid memories, and I hate them because when I relive those times I still cry. Perhaps I was naturally sensitive, perhaps I became sensitive because of all that happened after being idolised by my father and left quite suddenly with a mother who hated me? So much happened in such a short time, momentous things which turned my world upside down at the age of 7. They are always in my mind and do not ease with age.

Even so, in spite of all the beatings and rejection I never lost my spirit or sense of humour. When I left Ladywood for Upwood I took some positive things with me. In that servant's kitchen I would have the others in stitches as I told them about my other life. I would be the hawkers shouting their wares. The man who sold the bananas called 'A penny for two bananas' but it came out 'A fenny for chew-a-nanas'. And the coalman nicknamed Mucky used to shout 'c'Oal, c'Oal'. They helped to liven up hard times.

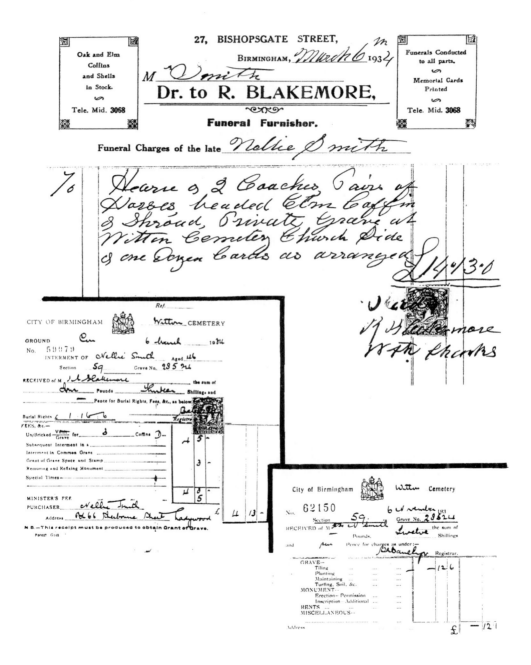

Victoria Road, Aston

I don't know how we got to Aston but it must have been by
tram, which I never liked because the rocking motion made me
feel sick. I can't describe my feelings as we swayed into a new
life. I remember feeling cold but most of that day is a blank,
as if I was under an anaesthetic when time stands still and is
lost forever. I was in a low condition when we arrived at
Aunt Kate and Uncle Harry's house.

Gran, my mother's mother who lived in Essington Street was
Aunt Kate's half sister. They shared the surname of Hudson but
had different mothers. So Aunt Kate was my mother's Aunt and
younger than Gran by fifteen years or so. She and Uncle Harry
had two surviving children, 11 year old Ken and teenage Rene.

It would be marvellous if I could say we were greeted like long
lost relatives, but again, I have no memory of arriving. I am sure
we were welcomed, but there would have been tension. We were
not close relatives and did not even know them very well. I had
visited my aunt when they lived in Catherine Street, but not
often, and Florrie would have been a stranger to them.

We would have gone to bed that night like a couple of voyagers
after an eventful trek, calm after the storm. I am sure we slept.
Next morning I woke up with a wet vest because Florrie was a
bed wetter and we slept together.

You can't get a lot in a carrier bag and I think we had a couple
each. We probably had a change of underwear but no nightwear,
since we slept in our vests or shimmies. Our only shoes were on
our feet and I had a coat. Soon after arriving in Aston I kitted
us out with new clothes from top to toe. It was great to see
her nicely dressed with her curly, blonde hair clean and tidy.
She would meet me from work and be so pleased to see me.

I settled fairly well in our new home but it took Florrie some
time, years in fact. And in the early stages of our new life I
began to have doubts about what I had done. Trams ran down
Victoria Road both west to Lozells and east to Cuckoo Bridge
by Aston Reservoir. They were noisy, and with our room at
the front of the house we often found it hard to sleep. Even
so, you can get used to anything if you have to, and Floss
and I had no option.

The transition from a three roomed back to back house to an eight roomed semi in what was looked on as a posh part of Aston was astonishing. It even took a little time to walk from room to room. Uncle Harry was a polisher, a hard and dirty job but well paid enough for the family to afford some space and comfort.

The houses were semi detached with an entry between each pair which lead to the back. At the front was a small, walled garden with a path to the front door. This was a solid Victorian door which was left open during the day to reveal a tiled vestibule and an inner door partly glazed with stained glass. This was attractive and let light into the hall which would otherwise have been gloomy. Off the tiled hall was the staircase and the front parlour, which was the 'best room' and the pride of the family where the piano was kept.

Hanging above the piano was a large picture of a woman resting on her elbow, fingers entwined, looking dolefully into space. It was said to be Mary Magdalene. A story attached to the picture had it that when the artist took a second look he was horrified to discover that he had given the lady only nine fingers, so promptly committed suicide.

Aunt Kate wanted Ken to learn to play the piano. Learning to play any instrument takes patience and dedication, but Ken had little of these qualities and his ideas were entirely at odds with his mother's. Even so, he showed willing and took an alarm clock to his practice sessions which was set to go off after fifteen minutes.

One day I was sitting with Aunt in the kitchen with the door open to hear Ken performing. Sounds were coming from the direction of the parlour and Aunt was looking very pleased with them. She got up from her chair to busy herself in the kitchen, forgetting her little concert pianist.

When she had finished what she was doing Aunt sat down again by the fire, than lifted her head and remarked that she could not hear the piano. I knew, I hadn't heard the piano for ages. Making her way down the hall she called 'Ken. Ken. What are you doing?' There was no sign of Ken but the window was open. The alarm had gone off and so had Ken, to kick a ball about with his pals.

Next off the hall was a room with French doors opening onto the yard which housed a billiard table, a gramophone and lots of records. I don't remember there being any books. Like our Mom,

Aunt Kate thought reading a waste of time. She would grumble if her daughter, Rene, was seen absorbed in 'Peg's Paper'.

The kitchen was small and comfortable, but with six people there at a time it was crowded. There was a black iron range on which the food was cooked, and from the oven came the most delicious fruit cake you ever tasted. Uncle Harry would say that a piece of Aunt's cake was better than any physic. She would never divulge the recipe and did not like you around when she was cooking, but was always pleased if you washed up. This was done in the scullery beside the kitchen which also served as the laundry.

At the back of the house was a yard, a private yard, where sports mad Ken would kick a football for endless hours. Beyond the yard was a long garden looking toward Aston Hall which was bordered on each side by tall mature trees.

The lavatory was outside, which was normal for the times, but it was ours' alone. Even people who lived in a posh house in a posh road had sheets of newspaper hanging from a nail on the wall. At Upwood they had bathrooms and indoor lavatories, in fact two of each, but they were for the privileged few. The servants, the common folk, had to cross the yard and use the familiar squares of newspaper.

Victoria Road was in a very convenient area. Just five houses away was the Victoria Picture House, which was expensive, but there was another one on Lichfield Road near Catherine Street. If you didn't fancy the film showing there you could nip down to Aston Cross by Rocky Lane to yet another cinema. Also in Victoria Road were the swimming baths, then by turning right at the top to the Albert Hall where you could dance your socks off for a shilling any Monday night. This was where Mr Joyce, the Master of Ceremonies, introduced girl to boy as Lady So and So and Sir Somebody or Something.

Lichfield Road was a good place to shop. Thompson's, the pork butchers, was very popular though it did not quite match Ward's in Broad Street. At Aston Cross the Co-op had a monopoly with the drawing power of 'divi'. In the corner by the Co-op stood a flower seller with his baskets where I used to buy a shilling bunch for my mother's grave.

Aston was more than sights and sounds; there were smells. Ansell's Brewery on the corner of Lichfield Road and Park Road competed with HP Sauce in the next road. On brewing days the steamy clouds of hops and yeast from Ansell's almost matched the pungent vinegar and spices of 'The Sauce'. There was also the small Smith's Brewery in Lichfield Road near the Station, but if could offer only weak olfactory competition to its mighty neighbours.

Floss started at a school in Gem Street, Gosta Green. She soon settled in and was very happy but missed her friend from Sherborne Street. Ken tried to get her interested in football but he kept putting her in goal where she let too many in. With scores of 50 - nil Ken won every time. When she married Floss found herself with a husband and six sons who were all Blues fanatics, so her weekends were chaotic. She never took to the game.

My Uncle got me a job where he worked at Aston Cross but I did not stay long, it was a stop gap until I found a job that paid better. From a basic wage of about 16 shillings a week [80p] I had to give Aunt Kate 14 shillings for my board and keep.

Before long I met the Smith twins, Rose and Lily, who lived in Church Lane at the junction of Victoria Road and Lichfield Road. They told me about Kynoch's in Witton where they had good conditions and light piecework, so I found myself a job there.

When work was goin well you might have a shilling or two more in your pay packet than expected. On these good weeks you sailed home on Friday nights on air, planning to go to town on Saturday afternoon to see what that extra couple of bob would buy. If you couldn't afford what you wanted you could try on hats in Lewis's, a wonderful free entertainment.

At this time Uncle Harry and Aunt Kate left Victoria Road and took a much smaller terraced house in Pugh Road. It meant less work for Aunt and, of course, less rent, but we were cramped. Floss and me shared a bedroom with Ken, while Rene slept in what was more or less a box room off it. Uncle and Aunt had the front bedroom. There were three rooms on the ground floor but no hall, so you entered the front room from the street. Next came the living room with the kitchen at the back and the WC in the yard.

Although the savings on rent and housework were welcome, there was another reason for moving. The house in Victoria Road was a sad reminder of a son who had recently died there. Arthur had been about 22 when he died in 1932, a terrible loss, and especially when added to the loss of Harold in World War I.

Moving house took me nearer to the Smith's where I was always made welcome. They were a big family with seven still living at home and three married daughters nearby. What fun we had in the Smith's back room and walking to work every morning with Rose and Lily, always laughing and joking over stupid, silly things. It was a good thing we didn't work on the same section.

Every Friday night we went to the Public Baths at Electric Avenue with a towel rolled round a bar of soap. You had to join the queue early or face a long wait. We couldn't wait to sit in a bath of lovely hot water, even though there was barely enough to cover our bottoms. When at last you got to the bathroom you would have undone all your buttons to save time, but dreams of a long soak were soon shattered by the attendant. She stalked the corridor knocking on each door and calling in a high soprano voice, 'Hurry along girls, there are others waiting'. You had to comply because she could pull out your plug. Walking home in the cold night air, your teeth would be chattering until you could get to the fire and a cup of cocoa.

In the slum clearance of the 1920s and 30s thousands of people were moved to the suburbs and our Public Baths became almost redundant. This migration did not happen overnight and some people waited years. The most needy were moved first according to the condition of their house, the facilities and how many people lived there. I knew a boy who slept in a basket under a table for want of space.

When at last people's turn came for a move to one of the estates it was very welcome. Instead of gas lighting with its dangers and the constant problem of broken mantles, they had only to flick a switch. They had cold water from *indoor* taps and hot too, heated by kitchen ranges with ovens big enough to take a Christmas turkey. The new houses meant a bathroom for every family. Forget the jokes about keeping coal in the bath, the bathrooms I encountered were holy places, shrines to cleanliness.

Lightning Fastners
1934/1939

The day I started work at Lightning Fasteners on the
Kynoch site in Witton I couldn't believe it was a factory.
The buildings were so light, clean and airy that they seemed
like a palace compared to some of the places I worked in.

My first job was on the assembly line and the section head,
Dolly Wetherly, showed me what to do. This was a simple
operation of drawing tapes with teeth on through a slider
attached to the bench and cutting off the length required.
Slipper fasteners for example, were just four inches long,
but fasteners for skirts were much longer.

I was very happy with my work. It was a bit repetitive but
no worse, I would think, than selling stamps at a post office
counter. Zip fasteners came in a variety of sizes and more
shades than the rainbow. At one time they had made a shade
of green which awaited a name. Some wag suggested Acock's
Green, followed by Barnt Green, Bartley Green and so on,
but it became 'Resida'.

In time I settled down to work on the section mysteriously
named, 'box-open-ends'. These were a brilliant improve-
ment on the whole brilliant idea of the zip fastner. Existing
fasteners opened at only one end because the two sets of
teeth had to be fixed permanently together, so they could not
be used at all on coats, for example. The 'open-end' meant
that the two sides of the zip could easily be separated and
reattached by putting the bottom stop into the box-end.

Our shop stood on the edge of the ICI Kynoch site with gates
onto Brookvale Road and the River Tame running alongside.
We were not allowed to stay in the works to eat our lunch, so
in nice weather a group of us would eat our sandwiches in an
area area behind the buildings, where there was grass, trees
and bushes.

One of the two buildings dealing with fasteners housed a
laundry where the finished articles were washed and dried in
large ovens. The girls in charge of this wet, heavy work wore
rubber aprons and wellington boots. They worked in soap suds,
steam and water for eight and a half hours a day at what must
have been the most unenvied job of all, but they went about

it singing and happy. On the whole Lightning Fastners was a very happy place to work and I still remember the girls.

Not everything that happened was happy. On one occasion a girl stood up and 'sissed' to catch the attention of another some distance away. Looking up, the second girl was confronted by a flying fastener thrown by girl No. 1. Luckily she caught it and no harm was done, but the boss had seen what happened and instantly dismissed the zip thrower with a sermon about the damage she could have done.

Near the Fasteners buildings and in its own grounds stood the house of the Chief Engineer, Peter Franks. It was later used as a management training school and eventually demolished to make way for another factory. There were other employees living on the site. A security officer and his family lived in a house at the gate of Lightning Fasteners and another by the entrance gates at Wellhead Lane.

The welfare of employees both on and off the site was important to Kynoch's and they provided ample sports facilities on the grounds, except for swimming, for which they had an arrangement with the baths at Victoria Road, Aston. Football was popular, with a George Butcher, who also worked on 'box-open-ends' and whom I came to know better, taking the Juniors every Saturday afternoon. My cousin, Ken Swash, was one of them. There was a cricket club, a swimming club of which I was once a member, and a tennis club.

The pavilion in the 1930s had the usual changing rooms but it was partly a social club where you could get a game of darts and play billiards. I had a few billiard lesson from my 'young man', George Butcher, when there were no other players at the tables. It was not thought right for ladies to play because of some of the positions you had to adopt. We didn't wear trousers then, but since our clothes were almost down to our ankles I have doubts about the real motive for the ban. Most of our courting was done in the pavilion with George playing billiards and me watching from the twilight on the hard leather benches. It was a cheap night out costing just a shilling to play, and I only drank lemonade.

Among the regulars there was Billy Carter whose wife was not happy for him to have a drink. She would bring sandwiches for his supper and he tried very hard to keep her to stay, but she would not even have a lemonade. At one time he persuaded her to sip his beer. She made such a fuss, calling him and his beer all sorts, but he just said, deadpan, 'Now you know what I go through drinking it'.

Mrs Carter then went home with Billy's sandwiches but returned with them shortly after. His first bite left him with a mouthful of bones, and parting the two slices he found the ribcage of a rabbit. Not a word was said by anybody. We just looked at each other waiting for the first titter, but it never came. Billy sat picking what meat he could off the bones.

In those days members of the company management staff would join the workers for a pint and a chat. Such was the atmosphere of the place, small and friendly. All that changed with the intensive alterations to the clubhouse in the 1950's and the introduction of one armed bandits.

During the winters a dance was held on Friday evenings at Kynoch's Perry Barr offices. This was always packed, perhaps because it didn't matter if you had no partner to dance with. If need be we girls would dance together to records of some of the best dance bands on a wind up gramophone, and all for 1 shilling.

There wasn't a Ginger Rogers or a Fred Astaire amongst us but we felt like them, always practising new steps to add to our repertoire. You had to be step perfect or you would be trodden on and end up with sore toes.

Alcohol was not served in ballrooms then so there was never any rowdiness. The entertainment finished at 10.00 pm and we hurried home because very few young people were allowed out after that hour.

I have always loved to dance and now, at 81, can still can dance a moderate quick step, a not too fast Cha-Cha-Cha and a stately Rhumba.

George did not take part because he was still going to Aston Technical College for two or more evenings a week to learn his trade as a tool maker. With evenings at the Tec and all the extra studying, he had no time for a misspent youth.

Celebrities visited Kynoch from time to time, including a leading lady - Dorothy Ward, and a Prince of Japan, a diminutive figure in a dark suit. In 1937 there was great exitement over the coronation of Edward VIII. Wherever possible bunting, union jacks and balloons were put up with each section on the works trying to outdo its neighbour. It was a sad day when we had to dismantle it because Edward the uncrowned king, had abdicated. I still have some souvenirs which had hung over the tool setters' bench, a silk union jack measuring 9" x 7" and a royal blue sampler. Held to the light, the centre panel shows a crown beneath the King's head in profile and the side panels the month and year, May 1937.

The Kynoch offices in Witton.

Ken Swash and Florrie Coronation Day 1937

The double bending section at Lightning Fastners 1936/37

Happy Campers

In late August each year Kynoch's organised camps for their employees aged between 14 and 18 years. We could all have a week in the beautiful Worcestershire countryside, the girls at Clifton on Teme and the boys some ten miles away at Tenbury Wells.

The cost for the week including transport and plenty of wholesome food was 14sh [70p]. It was wonderful value but still had to be earned and paid for out of pocket money. We paid by instalments, starting as early as January when our 6 pence per week would be entered on a card, or 1 shilling on a good week.

It made a cheap holiday because there was no opportunity for spending pocket money in rural Worcestershire and we didn't need many clothes. All we took was a couple of pairs of shorts and blouses, a pair of white pumps and a bathing costume for a dip in the River Teme which ran past the camp.

We were taken to the campsite by Kynoch lorries and on the Saturday morning assembled on the forecourt of the main offices at the Witton entrance. There were the moms and dads with some of the girls, carrying suitcases, giving advice and worrying whether they were doing the right thing in letting their offspring loose without them. Holidays then were family affairs, to go away alone or even with a friend was almost unheard of. The last plea as they climbed on the lorry would be, 'Send us a postcard'.

They were going away for one week's freedom but were expected to use some of that precious time going miles to find a post office in the depths of Worcestershire. Even so, they were the lucky ones, with parents to care about them.

To get everything ready for the campers a volunteer force was sent four or five days earlier. They unloaded lorries full of tents, cooking equipment, crockery, cutlery, lamps bedding, tables and benches. Then they had to haul and hammer and organise it all into a tented village to house sixty or seventy people sleeping six to a bell tent. There was a cooking area, store tent, cooks and officials' tents, first aid tent, latrines and a marquee for social events.

Helen and Florrie on a day trip to Rhyl in 1934.

Clifton on Teme 1935

Smith twins with Helen at the back.

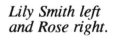

Helen with straw sack for a bed.

Lily Smith left and Rose right.

The only chore of the week was washing up, but in summer in a Worcestershire field it was not a chore. Someone would 'accidentally' splash water on someone else, which would lead to a battle of wet dishcloths. It ended when the water was all gone, the table was awash and we had to go for dry clothes.

Probably the most important person in the camp was the cook. The weather might be wet or dry, but a well fed camp is a happy one. Ernie Ball was cook at the boys' camp for a good many years. He was an ex-army cook, so they had a substantial and very good military menu which ran to rabbit stew and boiled beef with carrots, onions, dumplings and potatoes in rich brown gravy.

We swam in the river, played games and went for walks on nearby lanes, as happy as we could ever be. We had nothing to do and all day to do it in. There was no watching the clock and leaving half cups of tea in case we missed the tram to work. There was no bell to sound the start of the working day and no machines switched on. We we free of the nervy, nattering click-click-click of tape machines and the brain numbing thump-thump of power presses.

My sister Floss was not working at this time, but I managed to arrange for her to stay with a family living near the camp, where she had children a bit younger than herself for company.

Down in the Forest

After a couple of years I became too old for the camp. George's holiday was already taken care of because he was now an official at the boy's camp, but I had to think of something new. With the Smith twins, Rose and Lilly, and Rosie Beard, a close friend of theirs, I started to plan. Annual holidays at a price we could afford were not easy to find.

In most working families there would be little left over from the pay packet for such luxuries. The most they could hope for would be a day on the Lickey Hills or a paddle in the

'Reza' - Edgbaston Reservoir, with a bottle of tea and some bread and marge wrapped in the *Evening Mail*.

To be fair to the Lickey's, a day out there was a great event. The tram terminus in Navigation Street saw weekend queues long enough to creep far up Suffolk Street. On Bank Holidays you might stand for an hour or more.

It was worth the wait, and to get a seat on top in the open parts at the front or back was bliss. The lines ran down the centre of Bristol Road with trees lining each side. We rocked down an endless avenue of greenery to the clack-er-t-clack of the wheels, the wind on our faces, skimming past the big houses where the toffs lived and my Grandad used to do his tatting.

Yes, but we had been to the Lickey's and had a whole week to spend, so where to go? It had to be somewhere in the country accessible by train or Midland Red bus. By asking around we learnt of a Mr and Mrs Guest who took holiday makers at Far Forest, and they were within our price range.

We had never heard of Far Forest and it sounded a long way off. Nor had we ever heard of anyone spending a week in a forest, but it might be nice. The only forest we knew about was Sherwood Forest, so perhaps it was there. Without any real idea where we were going we booked for the first week in August.

Far Forest turned out to be a remote spot lost in the middle of the Wyre Forest, and it still is. We got as near as we could on a lurching bus from Kidderminster, then set out to walk the lanes 'just a couple of miles' to the Guest's house.

We had heard about country miles being measured as the crow flies. It's easy for him, he flies in a straight line with no luggage.

Looking back to when we were young we remember only hot, cloudless days, and it seemed especially so on that long afternoon. As we trudged to our holiday home we would have welcomed a cooling shower of rain. We often put down our cases to rest. These were not lightweight, modern cases and seemed to weigh more than the few clothes they held. We had packed only the shorts, blouses and white pumps from our camping days with a couple of frocks for evenings.

The lanes and paths we followed wound on and on seeming endless, going nowhere. We felt lost, never having been to the place and with nothing to guide us. Eventually we saw something in the distance, though at first we dismissed it as a mirage produced by wishful thinking. We knocked on the door of the cottage, a pretty little cottage in a garden blazing with colour, and it did not vanish.

From the little garden we took stock. All around were trees, trees, wherever we looked. There were trees surrounded by trees. I could not put a name to any one of them and I don't suppose the others could either, though the twins did have a tree at the bottom of their garden on Lichfield Road.

The lady who answered the cottage door soon put us on the right path to Mr and Mrs Guests' farm. Dragging our suitcases that final stage we asked each other how we had got so lost. We did not find the answer and I didn't care, we had arrived.

I had started in the morning with a sore throat which grew worse as the day wore on, and soon felt so ill that I had to go to bed. In fact I was too ill to get out of bed, could not swallow and had a high temperature. I was not short of visitors though. People would pop their head round the bedroom door asking, 'Feel any better?' This went on for about three days before Mrs Guest decided to call the District Nurse.

In the 1930s telephones were not to be found in every house, so someone probably walked miles to the nearest telephone box to get a message to the nurse. Eventually we heard that she was out on her rounds but would call as soon as possible. She arrived in the evening after a busy day, took a long look at my throat and left. I had a septic throat and a very high temperature. If there was no change within the next few hours I would have to go to hospital.

I don't know what was in the glass that Mrs Guest told me to sip. She said it would bring my temperature down and didn't leave me until I had emptied the old glass goblet. She told me later that this was very old and had been in her family a good many years, but that liquid was potent and would have given the same results in a jam jar. I don't know whether the goblet held any therapeutic qualities, but after a few more glasses of the strange liquid I began to perk up, so much so that there was no need to call back the nurse.

Mr Guest and children with Lily Smith on the wall.

Kidderminster Station

Wyre Forest 1936

▶ *Helen and Lilly*

The Smith twins with Joby

Half the holiday week had gone but my illness had not affected my friends' enjoyment too much. A crowd of Black Country lads were camping in the grounds of the house, so nobody had gone short of entertainment. We had a lot of fun between their dialect and our 'Brummagem'.

A regular visitor of the Guests was Joby, a lightly built Black Country man in his late 30s. He had a huge, sharp witted sense of humour and became the life and soul of the place. He presented himself every evening wearing his two tone shoes, pressed trousers, white shirt, and the first bow tie I had ever seen. For lounging about on the grass it was quite an outfit, especially worn with his pride and joy, a straw brimmer. Sadly, during a bout of tomfoolery, Joby's straw brimmer was knocked from his head and trodden on. He was terribly upset. I am so pleased to have a picture of Joby with Rose on his right arm and Lily on his left in the Guests' doorway.

Then, as today, presents were taken home to familys and, if your holiday money stretched to it, a friend or two. All Woolworth's branches carried a good line in 'Presents from Kidderminster', or wherever. Those 6 penny china souvenirs of prewar days are now collectors' items found only in antique shops, especially if bearing the trade mark, Goss.

Once more we came back to our workaday lives talking about our holiday adventures, the fun with new friends and the smashing food. Not that I had eaten very much. A stranger listening to us might have thought we had been half way round the world. We did not have to go so far for our excitement and pleasures, just a little further on from Kidderminster, a stone's throw from Brum. 'You'd like to go there next year? - I'll give you the address. Remember us to Mr and Mrs Guest, won't you? And Joby, he's bound to be there, he goes every year.'

Life and Times

I am not sure of the date that Uncle Harry suffered a heart attack and died, but we were all totally shocked. His death was especially hard to come to terms with because he was such a quiet, pleasant man. Uncle Harry had worked hard as a polisher on eight and a half hour shifts, standing all the time. Even so, in the evenings he usually found time to spend on his allotment in Moor Lane, Witton. Shortly after this sad event Aunt Kate moved house once more, I suppose to try to escape too many memories. I decided that it was time for Florrie and me to move on. George's parents took in Florrie and I moved in with their friends, the Flatleys.

We were beginning to hear of great unrest in Europe and about Hitler's persecution of Jews. Older people began talking of war because there was still a great mistrust of Germany. In contrast, things seemed to be getting better in my own world. Britain was getting back on its feet after the Great Depression, industry was picking up and there were more jobs, though they did not offer choice or prospects. However, there was another way for boys.

A boy with just an elementary education could try to get an apprenticeship with one of the big firms. George started as an apprentice tool maker. The first thing you had to learn was how to make a good cup of tea, so you were a dogs-body, and the wages were only about 10 shillings [50p] a week. But you would be taught a trade linked to a course at the Technical College. These usually ran at night after an eight and a half hour day's work, meaning years of hard grind with less time with your pals or girlfriend and hours of homework.

The Tec turned out first class tool makers. Starting as bench hands, they could progress to tool setters, charge hands and even foreman, with their own office. There was another avenue as well, and this was the way George wanted to go, to the drawing office. Draughtsman were like architects who designed the company's products and the plans for the tools to make them. From shop floor to drawing office seemed a tremendous leap for a lad like George, and some sceptics said it couldn't be done. They were wrong.

131

George and I had little enough time together, but life had its brighter side. The highlight of our week was usually the Saturday night pictures. We tried to sit upstairs in the 9 pennies [4.5p] half way down and in the centre, with George in the first seat. He liked to stretch his legs. Before you settled on a seat you made sure you could see over the heads of the people in the row in front.

After you had seen your favourite film stars you didn't notice the black night, or the rain, or how your shoes squelched and your coat collar clung dankly round your neck. The feet of Ginger Rogers and Fred Astair were poetry in motion and yours did not touch the ground.

To style our hair like Ginger Rogers we went through terrible ordeals. Wearing curlers as we imagined Ginger did every night, we tried to sleep with half a ton of steel between head and pillow and eyes bunged up with Vaseline to make our eyelashes grow long and curly. We never ever dreamed that both the beautiful hair and long, curling lashes were artefacts.

The Flatleys were buying their house at 113 Chester Road, which in the 1930s was very uncommon for ordinary working people. The price of £325 was a lot of money and the weekly mortgage payments were 11 shillings 3 pence [56p]. Most young couples had to live with relatives or friends until they could get a house to rent, so to buy one was a momentous decision.

To pay for it Mr Flatley was working long hours at Kynoch's foundry. He was, as people say, a grafter. He worked a week of day shifts followed by a week of nights. The night shifts paid more and I would guess his weekly wage would be in the region of £1.15.0 [£1.75]. The 16 shillings a week which I paid for my board and lodgings must have helped, but after paying the mortgage they would not have had much left to feed and clothe themselves and baby Alfie.

Borrowing large sums of money was just not possible for most of us. Even for more modest amounts, such as the price of a coat, you saved a little week by week until you had enough. The new coat would be worn only at weekends with your best frock, shoes, hat, handbag, gloves. After a season of wear the coat would not look so new and you would get tired of it, so you had to start saving again. The old new coat could then be worn for work. All this was laborious and slow but much better than depending on second hand shops. I felt that I was on the 'Up and Up' and worlds away from Sheepcote Street.

I was on piece work at Lightning Fastners so the incentive was there to keep at it. The more finished parts you weighed in at the end of the day, the happier you went home. On a good week I could pick up £1.12 shillings [£1.60]. This had to cover the Flatley's 16 shillings, leaving 16 shillings to cover clothes, bus fares and food at dinner time, though this was little more than a snack to keep us going.

We shared a small canteen with workers from the nearby Amal factory but only used it when we could no longer sit outside for lunch. For say, 3 pence, you could have a bowl of soup or a dish of rice pudding. Ruby Keeler liked hers with the skin on, but I didn't, so the order would be, 'Two rice puddings, please, one with and one without.' We could also get some fruit, buttered rolls, packets of biscuits and tea. Compared to the variety on any menu today ours must seem meagre. We survived, but I don't remember anybody in our crowd going on a diet to lose weight.

Living on little money was easier then in one way, because we were not bombarded with advertisements. We saw them only on posters, in newspapers and at the cinema, and they were pretty innocuous. Promises that lotions would 'make your hands as soft as velvet' were easily ignored. We did buy Pond's Cold Cream, and if you ever wondered about the slightly odd name, it was intended to protect your skin on cold and windy days. A little Vaseline on our lips prevented chapping and on our eyelashes enhanced growth, we thought. A little make up would be used at weekends, but never for work where a made up girl stood out like a sore thumb. I once heard my Aunt give her daughter, who was married and a mother, a terrible telling off for wearing lipstick.

There were rare and exotic exceptions. Kate Hawkins who worked on our section at Lightning Fastners not only used make up, she bleached her hair, and not very well. Not that Kate cared what anyone said about her. She lived life in the fast lane and to the full, always good for a laugh and a joke.

Friday being pay day, Kate would celebrate the night with a few G & T's or beer, it depending on who was paying. She would come to work on Saturday morning after catching the train from Walsall by a whisker. Having slept late she had not washed her face, so we saw her through the last night's smeared make up. Kate never managed to put her curlers in her hair before going to bed, if she had been there, so it looked slept in. The shoe fashion at that time was the Spanish heel, so Kate had a red pair. To see her trying to walk a straight line on four inch heels was hilarious, especially if she was feeling delicate from Friday night's festivities.

Kate was not the marrying kind and seemed to have no maternal instinct. A good time girl was Kate, getting all she could out of life, living every day and night to the full. Leaving her home in the dismal surroundings of Bridge Street, Walsall to take the 7.30 train for Witton each day, looking through the window onto the same bleak view, day in, day out for weeks, months years, Kate lived just for Friday night.

You may or may not have approved of Kate's approach to life, but it took a very independent spirit. For most of us 'Friday night was Amami Night' when we washed our hair and didn't go out. It was a ritual, liked boiled ham sandwiches for tea at Aunt Kate's.

Not far from Liverpool

Christmas had come and gone so the talk was once more of where do we go for our holiday? Well, said the Smith twins, as in one voice, Rosie Beard and a couple of her friends are talking about a week in the Isle of Man. What did I think about that? I thought a holiday abroad was a bit beyond my means and I did not fancy starting it by crossing the sea, even in a ship. I was frightened of water. We decided that I would think it over.

Going home on the bus I kept thinking about this proposed holiday. I knew the twins were keen on the idea. If I didn't go I was left with the prospect of stopping at home because George would be at camp.

After dinner at the Flatley's and the bedding of 18 month old Alfie, we sat by the fire. Mr Flatley was reading the

News of the World which he bought for the sport. He knew
a lot about sport and the paper certainly covered them all.
Some where highly unusual, especially when certain film
stars started telling their life stories. The games some of
them played, disgusting, we all agreed, but next Sunday
we had the *News of the World* again as usual.

Mrs Flatley picked up her knitting, switched on the wireless, and started clicking furiously on the other side
of the fireplace. Soon she got tired of the programme and
switched the the wireless off, and I took my chance to
mention the proposed holiday.

Did they know anything about the Isle of Man? Oh yes,
they had cats without tails and a motorbike race. The
geography of the British Isles had been sadly neglected at
school and I hadn't the faintest notion where the Isle of Man
was, but Mr Flatley knew - 'Its not far from Liverpool'. I
knew that at Liverpool they built big liners and that it was
'up there'. It was quite a way by train, but the journey by
sea wasn't too long, I was told. Nothing to worry about. I
felt quite lighthearted as I put in my curlers.

Next day it was all settled. We were going to the Isle of
Man. The posters promised a 'holiday of a lifetime' on a
sun drenched isle, but would we get on with the natives?
Being English and abroad the finer points of etiquette
must be observed at all times. I couldn't wait to see the
tailless cats.

'Our Mary has been to the Isle of Man', said the twins,
'So, she's going to book it for us'. There was a lot to be
done, first of all arranging lodgings where the deciding
factor would be the cost for a week's full board, then we
had to find the train fare to Liverpool and buy a steamer
ticket. How we had moved on, the Wyre Forest one year,
across the sea the next.

The train journey to Liverpool was fine, but waiting on the
Pier Head to board the steamer in lashing rain and a keen
wind off the Mersey was not.

Rose and Lily Smith, Maisie, Rosie Beard, Vera Moss and
I, we shuffled slowly across the quay with our luggage. A
long time passed and still we edged our way through the rain
towards the boat. I had bought a new navy blue hat for the

journey. The style was called the halo in which the brim turned back from the face, a watered down version of the Queen Mother's favourite style. Now it was being watered down further. Suddenly I found myself swaying and dizzy. The solid quay had been replaced by a bucking gangway. 'Never mind', I was assured, 'We're just about to get on the boat. You'll be alright then.'

I doubted this because the gangway was attached to the boat and the boat was heaving drunkenly up and down even while moored to the quay. To save money we had booked a night crossing. It was as well, because if I had seen the thrashing, rolling Irish Sea in daylight, no threat, promise or cajoling would have got me aboard.

In time we found ourselves on board and followed the crowd into a room which was already filled to bursting. Everyone had the same purpose, to find a seat and get warm. I remember the smell of hot oil and feeling sick. Lily had the brilliant idea, 'Let's go up on top, in the air. You don't ever get seasick if you're in the open.' I suppose it was better. If you were going to be sick there would be fewer witnesses, and you could just sort of hang over the rail and hope the wind was in your favour.

The twins and I stayed together on top, in the rain, and found some chairs to sit in. Suddenly mine slid down the deck and I felt extremely ill. When I opened my eyes I could see what I thought was the boat rearing up in front of me, so I shut them again. I don't know how long I lay there, wishing that the next wave would take me with it. Every so often, a voice, one of the sailors, would ask, 'Are you alright?' After a while the visits stopped; he was sick too.

Most of us were ill on that crossing, which was said to be one of the roughest nights ever. It took about six hours of wind, rain and darkness to reach the Isle of Man.

In the thin daylight people stood in knots on the Douglas quayside discussing their night at sea. 'That's the last time I'll come to the place,' some were saying, but I expect most of them had such a good time they forgot about it. I had heard of people turning green with sea sickness, and there on the quay was a woman with a pea green face.

As for me, apart from a night I would never forget I had been sick in my new hat which had shrunk in the rain. Having at last reached the Isle of Man I worried all week about getting back, and vowed never to come again. I never did, although I would fly there.

Our digs turned out to be in a tall, run down Victorian house. It seemed that we were going to share the place with about fifty other holiday makers. 'That's alright,' we assured the landlady, we didn't mind sharing a bedroom just for a week. In single file we dragged our cases up the stairs after her. On the landing she opened a door and stood back, motioning with a nod of her head. The first of our group walked in followed by the next, then another. The rest of us expected to be led to other rooms, but like a sheepdog rounding sheep into a pen, all six of us were herded into that room. She gave the last one a key, then retreated down the stairs.

The six of us, with our luggage, filled the narrow gap left between two beds. That grasping landlady knew only too well there was nothing we could do. We had no money to pay for anything else and every house and hotel on the island would be packed like hers.

Early on Saturday evening we set off to see what affordable entertainment Douglas had to offer. Apart from a day trip to Rhyl I had no idea what a seaside holiday town was like, and I was not prepared for crowds such as were milling around us. Everybody seemed to have the happy, holiday feeling and there was a lot of laughter. Suddenly from nowhere came a line of singing boys and girls, arms linked. As we moved aside for them I saw a face in the middle that I had not seen since leaving Ladywood, Ada Bishop. She was singing a very touching ballad about how, 'You don't get many pimples on a pound of pickled pork.' Her family had shown me great kindness when I stayed at their house just before Mother's funeral and shared Ada's bed. I have not seen her since.

Somehow we reached an area where the crowd thinned out. At a count, we were still six, so on we went to Derby Castle, the mecca for dancing and entertainment.

On the Sunday morning we joined a crowd of visitors to a place where an open air Christian service was held. None of us went to Church at home, yet here we were after a long walk, singing lustily the odd hymn we had learned at school. There must have been hundreds of people at that gathering. It was not exactly an unwritten law that you had to be there, but a suggestion was passed on from former visitors that it was well worth your time and effort. The time we spent and the energy used in the long walk there and back gave us an appetite for our lunch. It is one of the few things I remember of that holiday.

Another is having the great music hall star, Florrie Ford, waiting patiently while I tried to undo the knot in my hanky to get at our joint spending money. She had finished her performance, belting out songs which our Mom had known and I had grown up with, and was among the audience selling signed photographs of herself. I was as nervous as if she were the Queen. Florrie had been the pin up girl of the early part of the century and in 1938 was still a star, but she was no chicken and died soon afterwards.

Without transport we were confined to Douglas so we did not see much of the Isle of Man. We climbed Douglas Head a few times and watched ferries sail in and out. They brought and took not only passengers, but goods of every description for everyday living and cheap souvenirs for the tourists. How strange to think that all those oddment bearing the Arms of Man - actually legs, and Manx cats, were probably made in Birmingham. We also saw a real Manx cat

I bought only George a present, something so different, so unusual, that he couldn't possibly go through life without one. It was a little shirt on its own little hanger with this verse on the front: 'When your handkerchief is clean, Put it it where it can be seen, But when your handkerchief is dirty, Put it in this little shirtie.' George never really commented on this present; perhaps it was a little too sophisticated for him.

The sea on our journey home was like a mill pond, somebody said cheerfully. I didn't know a thing about mill ponds and I did not care if I never saw the sea again. It was a smooth crossing back to Liverpool, but my heart was in my mouth until I got off that ferry. Sixty years later I still feel ill at the thought of the night I crossed the Irish Sea to the Isle of Man.

War

I could hear Mrs Flatley coming up the stairs calling, 'Take care - I don't want to spill this cup of tea'. 'But I want to see Nen as well,' came Alfie's baby voice from behind her. It was a beautiful Sunday morning in September 1939, the sort of weather for walking in Sutton Park which was only ten minutes away.

Two year old Alfie and I often went to the park. He loved to see the riders cantering past in their knee high, black leather boots. However, we had not seen the park for a week or two because I had been in the Ear, Nose & Throat Hospital having my tonsils out, not a pleasant experience at the age of 22.

The situation in Europe was getting worse. Hitler's troops had invaded Poland on 1st September. The next day France and Britain issued a join ultimatum that Germany withdraw within twelve hours or we would be at war. To say there was a hush in the air was an understatement. The generation who had survived the 'War To End All Wars' were afraid. They remembered the men who marched to the railway stations singing, laughing and waving to their friends and relatives, and how many never returned. Some who survived came home maimed and secretly wished they hadn't, but they never talked of their experiences. Others couldn't talk about it because their minds had gone.

We knew there was trouble when the Ward Sister told us that the the hospital had been ordered to evacuate, keeping there only patients too ill to be moved. My operation had been three days earlier and apart from a sore throat, I was fine. I was brought home by ambulance with orders to stay in bed for a few more days, hence my cup of tea in bed.

There was no banter from 'Nurse Flatley' that morning. I usually got, 'And how long are you thinking of stopping in bed, working me to death', etc. Today she opened the window so that I could hear the news on the Pemberton's wireless from next door.

The neighbours had opened their sitting room window and turned up the volume on their wireless so that I could hear

the announcement by the Prime Minister, Neville Chamberlain.
I heard the husband of the woman who had offered sympathy to
my mother after Tommy's death explain that Germany had not
responded to the ultimatum and that '.... we are at war with
Germany'. There was no cloud in the sky that morning of
3rd September 1939.

Military movements began very soon after Mr Chamberlain's
grim announcement. George was with me on my first outing
since the operation when we saw lorries carrying heavy tanks
south down Chester Road. I stood still and cried, George
made no comment. Neither of us spoke but we knew our
lives would change. We just walked on, arm in arm, along
Court Lane to his home in Tedbury Crescent for tea.

All through that Autumn it became apparent that there would
soon be changes, but for the time being life continued in a
weird normality. All around us troops and equipment were
moving. But apart from a British Expeditionary Force
landing in northern France and sporadic air attacks on
shipping, there seemed to be no fighting.

Limited and low key conscription had actually started before
war was declared, in April 1939. George's brother Bill was a
Signals Corps sergeant in the Territorial Army. Some referred
to the 'Terrors' as the Saturday Afternoon Army, but now they
were already mobilised.

George and I got engaged at Christmas 1939, though he said
we would not get married during the War. I understood his
reasoning. He said if he was wounded and came home unable
to work again it would be a burden for me. I understood the
logic but did not agree with it, so I kept my thoughts to
myself.

I moved jobs for a better paid one at Lucas's in Great Hampton Street. Being engaged to be married meant you had to
save as much as possible. The next pay day I went into the
post office in Great Hampton Row and deposited what I could
afford. It would only have been a few shillings, but it was a
start.

We did a lot of window shopping. I fancied a 'Queen Anne'
bedroom suite in the Times Furnishing shop at the Bull Ring.
I have forgotten the price, but I knew it was like asking for
the Crown Jewels.

Helen 1940

George and Helen early 1940.

Butchers left to right:
Reg - Fleet Air Arm
George - Royal Air Force
Bill - Royal Corps of Signals
Father.

'I've joined up' he said. George and I were walking along Erdington High Street one Saturday morning. All around us was hustle and bustle with busy mothers on the lookout for a bargain. Children were being told 'I can't afford it this week'. A baby throwing its rattle out of a pram for the umpteenth time was threatened, 'If ya do it again, I'm gonna leave it'. 'No you won't,' thinks the child, 'You'll pick it up.' And she does.

In the middle of Erdington High Street he tells me. 'What have you joined?', I asked. 'The Air Force. I want to be a pilot', he said. 'What for?' He answered quickly 'I want to paddle my own canoe'.

I did not grasp the real significance of his words at the time and lightheartedly replied that Air Force blue would suit him. I could have 'blarted my eyes out' there in the street. The thought of George going away had not entered my head. I thought in time he would be called up, but to volunteer, and for the Air Force.

There had been soldiers in our family. My Father was in the Army twenty one years, Uncle Tom had been in the Warwickshire Regiment and Uncle Jim in the Hussars. All through the First World War Uncle Ted was on mine-sweepers and in all served twenty one years in the Navy. My brother Ted was seven years in the Dorset Regiment, mostly in India. He was on the reserves list so would be among the first to be called up. Here we were, a new generation, babies of 'The War to end Wars' being trained to fight the next.

The first sign of war to affect everybody without exception was the Blackout. Woe betide anybody who erred and showed even the smallest sliver of light at night. The street warden's thundered command, 'Put that light out', would shake the blackness. In the strange lull of those first few months of the war there were no enemy planes, but it was as well we got used to the idea. When we could hear their engines there was often someone who thought he knew better than the warden and say, 'It's one of ours', meaning, 'You're being too fussy'. He could tell by the drone of the plane's engines it wasn't a Jerry, until the first bomb hit the ground.

'Have you got your torch?' 'Have you got your gas mask?' were questions we lived with for the next five long years.

142

Even the hand torches had to be masked. They gave only enough light to show just beyond our feet and guide us to the kerbstone. You learned to be vigilant to avoid accidents but if you suddenly collided with someone in the dark it could be funny. Strangers in the night would chuckle, never even seeing each other's faces, and a voice would trail away - 'Good night'.

Unlike during the First World War, the Government imposed a rationing scheme for food and other essentials devised by Lord Woolton. As in George Orwell's *Animal Farm,* all animals were equal but some were more equal than others and got a bigger share. It depended on who you knew and how much you were prepared to pay for extras on the black market.

The Phoney War

The period of weird calm that opened the war continued for months. Poland had fallen by early October and there were naval actions, such as the sinking of the German pocket battleship Graf Spee, but Britain itself was not attacked and life just went on.

It was unreal, but this interval gave the Government some time to organise and mobilise. This involved not just the armed forces, which were conscripted, but the work force as well. From farmers to factory workers, everyone was organised to produce essentials, particularly the weapons and ammunition with which to fight a ruthless and inhuman dictator. How terrible the enemy was we learnt only years later when the concentration camps were liberated.

There was a shuffling of jobs as women took over work in offices, shops and factories which men were leaving to join the armed forces. From public transport to farming, women appeared everywhere.

Many girls joined the Land Army, others, like Princess Elizabeth joined the Army Auxilary Training Services (ATS), the Women's Royal Air Force (WRAF) and the Navy (WRENS).

Poppy Scoltoch joined the WRENS imagining she would
work among sailors, I think she fancied the head gear.
The sailors would have like that because Poppy looked
remarkably like the film star, Joan Crawford. In fact
she became a galley slave at a kitchen sink in some
naval establishment and never went further than
Portsmouth.

Everybody was expected to do their bit in one role or other.
Women who had never worked before were on munitions,
examining twenty five pounder shell cases beside me. Some
of them only worked part time because they were old enough
to be our mothers, but they got on with it and mucked in.

One of these ladies smoked. At least, she lit a cigarette,
put it between her lips and allowed it to smoulder, the white
ash growing longer until it almost met her lips. Then she
removed the butt, lit another cigarette from it, clamped
it in her mouth and carry on working.

Before long we had news that a coalition government had
been formed with members from all political parties. More
important, on 10th May 1940 Winston Churchill became
Prime Minister. It was 4th June when he made his epic
speech and it rallied us for the years ahead. He promised
us only blood, sweat and tears before we gained victory.
We would fight them in the streets, we would fight them
in the fields, in the air, on the seas, etc. It was a wonderful, unifying boost to morale which lasted for years,
and every one of us backed him with our lives.

How odd to learn over forty years later that the voice we
heard had not been Churchill's, but that of actor Norman
Shelly, better known as Larry the Lamb in Toytown. They
were the Prime Minister's words, but read from a copy of a
speech he had delivered that day to the House of Commons.

He made other great and inspiring speeches that gave us
the will to win. We were not going to lose. We babies of
that other war knew about 'them Jerries' from stories told
by fathers, uncles, brothers and sisters, and this time we
civilians were all involved too. Of course, we had no idea
how tough it would be, or how long. Some were boasting
that it would be over in no time. We, Britain, would
pulverise the enemy in no time. Well, eventually we did,
with a great deal of help from the Americans, but at the
beginning it was all bluff.

Churchill knew a lot of things that we did not know. Britain was not equipped to fight a war, which is why we could do nothing effective about Poland. And after France fell to the Germans in late June 1940 we were on our own. The RAF was only two thirds the size of Hitler's Luftwaffe and our Army a fraction the size of the Wermacht.

Churchill also knew something much worse in August 1940, something so appalling that it was made known only to the cabinet. Britain would be bankrupt within three of four months with a complete collapse of British power and the means to fight. We were to become virtually an American dependency.

We did not know all this, and had we done so I am not sure that it would much have affected our mood. In those first, strange months industry worked round the clock for seven days a week. As day shifts clocked off, night shifts clocked on, working eleven hours with a short break for lunch. You ate what you had with you or went without.

I did nights voluntarily for sixteen weeks without a break. Changing from night to day working could be upsetting to the system, so I chose to carry on. When you arrived home the first thing you needed was sleep, but when you awoke, usually in the early afternoon, you had to go to the shops and trust to luck getting something to eat.

You didn't really go shopping so much as hunting for anything available. I remember going to Erdington Village with Gwen, daughter of the house where I was living, to see what we could scavenge for our tea. It turned out to be a cow heel. I knew of tripe and other offal, but had never heard of cow heel. We bore it home laughing, but boiled for a while with a few potatoes and carrots it made quite a good hot meal.

On Sundays I was sure of a good dinner at the Butchers' because my mother in law was a smashing cook. What she could produce from a rabbit or a veal knuckle had to be eaten to be believed.

Life was getting hard for the housewives who had to juggle ration books of coupons to buy any everyday thing. In the past when they got home from the shops the first thing they did was to put the kettle on. Now the first thing was to look in the tea caddy to see if they had enough tea.

Queuing became a way of life and a habit. In fact you would often join the end of a queue without knowing what was being sold because the queue itself showed there was something you wanted. Too often you would shuffle slowly towards the shop door only to hear the shop keeper shout, 'No More'.

One memorable invention was Woolton Pie, named after the Minister of Food, Lord Woolton. The great comedian, Tommy Handley, made it a sort of national institution with his endless jokes about it. Woolton Pie used no meat, which was scarce and rationed, but lots of root vegetables which were not. You cooked any available mixture of potatoes, parsnips, swede, carotts and so on, laid them in a pastry base with an onion or two, if you could get them, put on the pastry lid and baked your creation in the oven. Served with a gravy and any green vegetables you could find it was quite tasty and filling.

In April 1940 George left for his first RAF posting, which was in Norfolk under canvas. He was now officially, G.F. Butcher A.C.2 V.R. No. 1167595. I never need to look up that number, I wrote it so many time that I could never forget it.

We learnt in May 1940 that the Expeditionary Force was being evacuated from Dunkirk under Operation Dynamo. Even if the soldiers had had enough efficient weapons, many were mere lads who had only been in the army a few months. The only guns they had ever seen fired had been in booths at the Onion Fair on the Serpentine ground. In any case, a gun was of little use when you were up to your neck in water being straffed by German aircraft. Now they were targets like those fun fair ducks, praying that they would make it to one of the boats.

Every kind of craft crossed the Channel for the rescue, ships, steamers, fishing boats, rowing boats, anything that would float to hold even one or two men. One of the first was an Isle of Mann ferry. That flotilla of small vessels crewed by very brave men were also targets for the dive bombers, yet they sailed on, back and forth, between the French and English coasts until they too had to retreat. A great number of men were saved, 220,000 British with 120,000 French and Belgians, many were killed and the rest became prisoners of war. We lost 200 ships, 177 planes and all the Expeditionary Force's heavy weapons.

Ruby Keeler's boyfriend, Sam Rogers, was taken prisoner and it was months before his parents knew whether he was alive or dead. Ruby's granny knew though. He was alive because the cards said so. She would lay them out on the table time after time, and always the same story emerged. He was alive, but enclosed and unable to get out.

Of course, the story could have been the wrong one, but it was so heartening to watch that old lady turn up the cards and proclaim, 'He is alive', with such conviction. Ruby's face would light up, she believed her gran. I wasn't there when the news came that Sam was alive but a prisoner, but I would like to have seen gran's face. 'I told you so. But then, you don't believe in the cards, do you?'

Tied in Erdington

Norfolk was a lucky posting for George. On short leave passes he would thumb a lift on a Birmingham bound lorry and catch a tram from Steelhouse Lane to Stockland Green. Even so, we did not have a great deal of time together due to my working hours, and George was not in Norfolk for long. He had only entered the first course of training to become a pilot and to 'paddle his own canoe'.

George's first full week's leave was due in September 1940 and with six weeks to go he wrote telling me we would get married as near my birthday as possible, the 25th September. We settled on Saturday 21st. Without the help of George's mother and sister, Doreen, I don't know how I would have managed all the arrangements for the type of wedding we wanted.

First we arranged for the banns to be read at Erdington's Parish Church, St Barnabas's. The reception was left in the capable hands of Mr Joe Bradford and his wife. 'Gentleman Joe' had once been captain of Birmingham City but was then manager of the Stockland Green Hotel.

The cake presented quite a problem because all the ingredients were rationed. However, Birmingham Co-op had an ingenious alternative. A square cardboard box was dressed up as a most realistic cake, which seemed to be covered with white icing and trimmed with silver leaves. On top

147

*113 Chester Road,
New Oscott.*

Wed.

*St Barnabas's church,
Erdington.*

stood a silver vase holding a posy of white flowers. Even better, when the vase was removed it lifted a lid to reveal tiers of individually wrapped portions of rich fruit cake, each with its own silver decoration, spray, horseshoe, etc.

Purcell & Betts, an old established firm of photographers from Aston Road took the pictures. We could have four poses only because film was rationed to favour RAF reconnaissance planes. In our four were a bridal group and one of family, relatives and friends. They all look so happy and smiling, with ladies in new frocks and little Alfie Flatley in his new outfit. Actually Alfie is not happy and smiling because he didn't think much of being photographed. From that group of about forty people, only a handful are still alive.

Mr Flatley gave me away, and in the business of pushing the bride into the hired car he forgot to close his front door. They found it when they returned home at about 11.00 pm, but everything was as it had been twelve hours previously. Mrs Flatley loves telling that story, which always ends, 'Well, we'd got nothing to pinch'.

It was nearly midnight when George and I left the reception for our new home. As we waited for a No 11 bus at Stockland Green the sirens started to wail. Fortunately a bus came or we would have spent the night in an air raid shelter.

George had not yet seen where we were to live, a sitting room and bedroom with use of kitchen and bathroom ('no washing to be hung out on Sunday') at 16 shillings a week. It was the house of Frank and Lily Wallington in Deaken Road, Erdington. Frank was away in the Army, Mrs Wallington was away because she spent weekends with her mother at a cottage in the Cotswolds. Their daughter, Gwen, lived there but was on nursing duty at the hospital.

We let ourselves into the empty house. I knew the layout, in daylight, but now everywhere was pitch black. Groping along the hall to find the door to our sitting room, I opened it and automatically reached for the light switch. 'PUT THAT LIGHT OUT', yelled a voice from the road.

Boom, Boom, thundered Big Bertha from her site nearby, an awesome sound that seemed to come from the bowels of the earth. The enemy was up there and heading towards Birmingham. Big Bertha was warning them not to come too low.

I groped my way back to the front door where George was still standing. Finding strange rooms in the dark was bad enough, never mind hunting for an air raid shelter in the back garden. Since we couldn't stay in the hall all night, I gathered my wedding dress over one arm and we blundered upstairs.

I found my way to the bedroom window to draw the blackout curtains. From panic or stupidity I yanked too hard and they fell down. The ceiling light was covered with a cloth to give a very small beam, so I drew the ordinary curtains thinking they would be sufficient. Then George switched on. 'What do you think you're playing at?', screamed the warden, not too kindly I thought.

I draw a veil over the early part of 22nd September 1940. When light dawned it was the second day of what was to be a long marriage.

The Blitz

We endured many hardships over the next five years, but for me the Blitz period of nightly bombing raids was the worst. It lasted from September 1940 and May 1941, but one particular night in late 1940 will stay in my mind as long as I live. There was a particularly heavy raid over Birmingham on 9th November so it might have been then.

A little before 7.00 pm I caught the No. 2 tram at Six Ways, Erdington to start my night shift at Lucas's. We had reached Aston Cross when the air raid sirens started their dreadful moan. The driver stopped the tram to ask if anyone wanted to get off and go to a shelter. Some people were terrified of the raids.

There were few passengers at that time of night and perhaps four or five people got off. The driver then asked asked who wanted to go to town, and there was myself and another traveller who were going to work. 'Right,' said the driver, 'Then I will take you.'

The long fingers of searchlights reached back and forth across the sky as they tried to catch enemy aircraft in

their beams. They were dropping high explosive and
incendiary bombs while anti aircraft shells burst around
them like a nightmarish fireworks display. I prayed that
the tram driver who risked his life for us got home safely.

From the terminus in Steelhouse Lane I ran to Snow Hill
Station where I had to catch a bus. One was just leaving
for Smethwick or Oldbury, the conductor reached out to
drag me aboard and the bus careered like a drunken racing
car down Snow Hill and along Great Hampton Street to stop
right outside Lucas's. I don't remember paying a fare. The
big factory gates were closed so I hammered on them with
my fists. 'Ooh is it?', demanded a voice from the other.
side. 'It's me.', I shouted back. 'Ooh's me? Wat's ya
name and number?'

Stepping through the wicket gate, I was confronted by a
line of fully equipped Home Guards. I had volunteered for
fire watching so I ran up the stairs to join the other two
girls who formed our team. We took our places in a shelter
not much bigger than a telephone booth which was in the
middle of a huge floor, three stories up, filled entirely
with dozens of monstrous, black machines

Here we waited for action with stirrup pumps and buckets
of water and sand, though a fat lot of good they would have
been if a bomb had hit Lucas's.

Ours was a very small part. The heroes were those people
fighting the fires and rushing the injured to hospitals, the
nurses, doctors and ambulance men in the middle of the
carnage working till they dropped. Bus and tram drivers
still asked if there was anyone who wanted to go to town.
That night we all felt, perhaps for the first time, that our
backs were to the wall and the fight would be desperate.
And it made me and millions of others the more determined to pay back Hitler.

Lucas's nightwatchman kept us informed of the fires burning
all around the City Centre. I went out on to the fire escape
with him. We were facing Snow Hill Station and looking over
to the Market Hall. St Martin's Church was surrounded by fire
with everything ablaze but the spire still standing. The dawn
showed the results of eleven hours of destruction and death,
a devastated city. Miraculously there was little damage St
Martin's but only skeletal ruins remained of what had been
the heart of old Brum.

After that awful night George ordered, 'You come off nights'. My next job was working for the Chief Inspector of Armaments, Woolwich Arsenal, at a shadow factory known as Hughes's behind the Bagot Arms in Pype Hayes. This job was so much nearer to home that I saved money on fares and it had the added advantage that I only worked days. We were issued with a uniform of khaki overalls with brass buttons which were stamped with a shield held by two lions. I still have two of them.

The machinery was at the back of the building and from there the shells were passed to us inspectors to stamp with government numbers and figures. Then they were packed into ammunition cases ready for dispatch.

As the fighting in the North African desert to secure the Suez Canal turned in our favour, some of us CIA personnel were transferred to special work at IMI Witton. We would be working on a highly 'hush, hush, don't ask questions' product. For me it was a move nearer home.

A map on the wall of our room showed the progress of the North African campaign. Between November 1940 and late 1942 British and Commonwealth troops had first charged west from Egypt driving out the Italians, then been driven back east by Rommel to within reach of the Suez Canal. By the Autumn of 1942 Montgomery's Eighth Army was driving the exhausted Germans west again, as shown by a marker.

We were most impressed when some of His Majesty's top ranking officers came to inspect us and to divulge the secret of the component we were working on. It was part of the PIAT gun, a powerful weapon capable of penetrating tank armour. We were told that the initials stood for Pierson Infantry and Anti Tank weapon. It was forty five years before I knew what the thing looked like from a picture in the *Daily Mail* for Thursday 23rd July 1998.

When we left Hughes's we were presented with a certificate headed Woolwich Arsenal and thanking us for our services. I was offered a shell case but refused, saying I didn't need any reminders of the war. Many years later we were given one which had been made into an ash tray. The marks on the base read:
>   1Y: PR Mk 2 LOT I.C.I. S 1945.
It makes a good door stop.

Endpiece

I would like to end this book, the long and not very cheerful story of the first part of my life, with a little verse which for years has acted as a book mark in my Bible. It sums up the way I look back on it all and my feeling of having got through.

For all the heartaches, and the tears;
For gloomy days, and fruitless years,
I do give Thanks - for now I know,
These were the things that helped me
                                    grow.